Simple Parenting
Raising Confident *and* Cooperative Kids

D0951247

CHUCK & SHERRY QUINLEY

Medialight Productions, USA
3444 Hampreston Way NW
Kennesaw, GA 30144

For information about bulk purchasing please contact:
simpleparentingbook@gmail.com

ISBN 978-0-9802429-1-1
Printed in the USA

We dedicate this book to the ever-growing Tribe of Quinley.

Andrew, Jacki, August and Reese

Kristin & Jason

Nathan & Rebekah

Jessica & Ben

Brooke
Julia

You are the "arrows in the hands of a mighty warrior" that the Bible talks about. Each of you has a mission to accomplish in your lifetime and we see you already walking in that direction. We are proud of the way you choose people over possessions and mission over money.

We have raised you to be lights among the nations and we are proud to see your light shining onto the lives of all your friends. You have the bravery, confidence and poise that causes others to look to you for leadership. We know that you will provide it for them.

Thank you for loving us and for submitting to us and allowing us to do the job of parenting you to the best of our ability. We have not been perfect, but we gave it all we had. We have held nothing back from you that was for your good.

May the Lord grant each of you many children of your own and may all of you surpass us in goodness, love and impact on this world, until He comes.

We love you,
Dad & Mom

ACKNOWLEDGEMENTS

Our thanks to my mother, Dorothy Quinley, for proofreading this book patiently even after I kept making changes that caused her to have to redo the work repeatedly. Thanks Mom!

We thank also our son, Andrew, for acting as our marketing agent. Your counsel regarding the new world of e-publishing has been invaluable.

We probably wouldn't have gotten around to writing at this time but for the constant encouragement and harassment of Greg Clark, our dear friend of many years. Thanks, Greg, for riding my case until I got it written! Every writer needs a friend like you.

Thanks to Ria Bagatsing, who created the charts for the book. You can reach her at riabagatsing@gmail.com.

Finally, huge thanks to Rory Morales-Gutierrez who crunched the layout of text, photos and cover under a tight deadline. Her work speaks for itself. You can reach her at aurora@morealis.com.

Sherry and I wish to express our deepest appreciation to both sets of our parents, Warren and Dorothy Quinley and Sam and Audrey Smith, for being solid parents for us and for giving us the treasure of being raised in healthy homes. You modeled so much of what we have written in these pages.

PREFACE

The Greeks said that you cannot measure the happiness of a man's life until you see how it ends. Parenting is like that. You can't tell how well you have done until your kids leave your home and establish lives and families of their own. Everything you do for them while they are under your care is done in preparation for that day. Then you can watch them functioning as adults and you'll see how well you've prepared them.

Sherry and I have been blessed with six wonderful children. We didn't plan to have so many, but once they started coming our life got better and better. We just never wanted to close the door on childbearing. That decision set the course of our lives. Our friends have watched from the sidelines and have urged us for years to write a book about all we were learning through the opportunity to experience parenthood six times.

Initially, we were just too busy raising kids to write a book about it. Then they started hitting their teens one-by-one and it just seemed right to finish the task of launching them all first before writing.

If we have a fear in the writing of this book it's that we might give the artificial impression that our family is more perfect than it truly is. Every family is a flawed human creation. Despite our best efforts, ours certainly is. I can honestly say that I doubt we've ever met a family without some trace of dysfunction. This is true in even the healthiest of families. We're just flawed and it affects everything we do. The good news is that a family doesn't have to be perfect in order to work.

Sherry and I would never claim to have done all things well as parents, but this year our last little bird has flown the nest to go to college, and so far nobody is in prison. So, it seems safe now to write this book we've been nursing for years.

We don't even claim to be parenting experts. We doubt that there is such a thing. What we offer you here is our handwritten playbook. Our lessons aren't from a psychology experiment. They are from the real world, our world. We have been parents with kids at home for a span of thirty years. We tried things that worked and a lot that didn't. We've learned from our mistakes and we've also made some great discoveries along the way.

We're calling this book, "Simple Parenting." We aren't saying that parenting is easy. It's not. Simple is the opposite of complicated.

Parenting is not always easy, but it isn't all that complicated. Most parents in history have actually been illiterate, so it's clear that we can master it no matter how much educational equipping we may or may not have. There is a natural order that parenting follows throughout a child's life, a workflow that changes as the child grows older and becomes more intellectually and emotionally mature. If we can simplify our objectives and just focus on a single outcome in each stage, then "the power of one" kicks in, the world slows down a bit, and shaping a family becomes more manageable.

The great thing about God's design for parenting is that a child's development is strictly sequential. There is no need to worry about third grade issues while your child is in kindergarten. No need to try and "advance them" by massive leaps so they'll be ahead of others. Just enjoy and celebrate each day and make sure that you keep the main thing, the main thing. Keep it simple.

We are excited to share with you the things that have worked so well for us. We do this in hopes that your family can avoid needless mistakes and take advantage of some secrets that took us years to discover. Although the principles you'll find inside cover the whole span of parenting, our target is to give sound counsel for those with children below fourteen. Results improve greatly when you apply these truths to younger children than those just a few years from leaving home.

We have a personal motive for writing this book too. By now, our children are having kids of their own, so we want to help them and their friends (who seem like our kids too) succeed as parents by letting them in on the behind-the-scenes work that went into raising them to be so healthy and competent.

Sherry and I could die now and be satisfied with the quality of our lives because we see strength in all of our children. We want you to feel the same way after your children leave you.

As a final note, I will say that while I, Chuck, function as the scribe in this work, the content in this book flows from both Sherry and myself. We have hammered it out together in the crucible of life for thirty years. In conversation and in counseling we have shared certain pieces of this content, but this is the first time we have tried to draw it all together into an intelligible package. We hope you will find encouragement and insight from your reading. We welcome your comments at Quinley.com.

Blessings,

Chuck and Sherry Quinley

Atlanta, GA - April 21, 2014

FOREWORD

I'll never forget that day in 1985. Six months into my first year as a missionary in the Philippines — on my never-ending quest to figure out how to impact a massive city of millions —   I attempted to make an appointment with the pastors of the five largest churches in Manila. Only two agreed to meet with this new kid on the block. My interview with a gray-haired pastor of a dynamic church of eight thousand still haunts me thirty years later. I showed up for the meeting expecting to learn about reaching a city, but instead I left with a very different lesson.

Notebook and pen ready, I asked the veteran missionary and pastor how his church had reached so many Filipinos. He soberly looked me in the eye and asked, "Are you sure you want a big church? There's a great price to pay." Already on the edge of my chair, I leaned forward and assured him that I was ready and willing to make any sacrifice to do what God had called me to do in the Philippines.

He continued, "Leading this church has cost me my family." I saw sadness in his eyes and voice as he told me his tragic story, admitting that his adult children wanted nothing to do with his church or ministry. When his story ended, I had no idea what to say. We both sat in an awkward thirty-second silence that felt like an hour.

Deborah and I didn't have children yet, but I walked out of this pastor's office vowing not to do family, church, and ministry this way. My mind was racing. As I got in my car, I prayed a desperate prayer: "Father, help me! We don't have kids yet, but one day we will, and there has to be a way to win this city without losing our family in the process. Show me a better way to serve you."

Not long after this gut-wrenching encounter, I was reading Hebrews. God seemed to speak loud and clear when I got to the part about Noah in Hebrews 11:7 — "By faith Noah, when warned about things not yet seen, in holy fear built an ark TO SAVE HIS FAMILY." (Emphasis mine.)

Consider the account of the same story in Genesis 7:1. "The Lord then said to Noah, 'Go into the ark, you AND YOUR WHOLE FAMILY.'" (Emphasis mine).

Noah fully obeyed God's call. His sacrificial obedience saved his family and the world. But God expected Noah to get on the boat with his family, not to leave his family behind. Too many leaders today leave their family behind in the process of obeying God and saving the world. It doesn't have to be that way.

Whether we're called to a grass hut in an African village or to a glass tower in a mega-city, pursuing the call of God always involves sacrifice. But it doesn't matter if we're called to ministry or business, we're not supposed to sacrifice family for ministry or career.

Most people really want to have strong families. But few actually know how. We instinctively know when something isn't right, but we have no clue how to fix it. We've got a lot of questions, but few answers. Chuck and Sherry give some great answers in this book.

Lest anyone misunderstand, let me be clear that I'm not advocating perfection. There are no perfect parents, no perfect families, and no perfect kids. What I'm talking about is having proper priorities and proper values. Like Noah, we must save our family first.

Anyone who knows the Quinley tribe knows that they're not perfect (who is?), but family is at the top of their priority pile.

My family and the Quinley family first connected in Manila through Little League t-ball. Chuck and I coached opposing teams. As our kids grew up, our families only grew closer. The more time one spends with the Quinley tribe, the more their love for Lord, their love for life, and their love for one another just rubs off on you.

I'm glad Chuck and Sherry finally wrote this book. I had the privilege of reading an advance copy on a recent Manila to Nashville flight. I love the title, Simple Parenting, and I love the content and spirit of the book. It suggests that no matter who you are or where you've come from, you can raise confident children who love Jesus and follow His calling for their lives. Chuck and Sherry certainly have. I invite you to learn from them (and their six kids) as they share stories of success, failure, and faithfulness in parenting.

I wish this book had been available twenty-eight years ago when our first son was born. As soon as Simple Parenting is available, I plan to give a copy to my son and daughter-in-law, who are raising our first grand-daughter (now four months old). I hope you will not only read this book, but buy one or two for some young parents who are trying to figure out how to raise a Godly family.

Steve Murrell

President, Every Nation Churches and Ministries
Founding pastor, Victory Manila

TABLE OF CONTENTS

*"As a man thinks in
his heart, so is he."*

SECTION ONE Foundational Concepts

In order to live as an effective parent you will need to take on a
new mindset. Up to this point you have been flying solo or living
in the happy, simple world of a couple in love. Parenting is an
entirely different life. Engaging it powerfully requires that we
change our expectations on what our days will be like during
this season. Without a change you will likely become a frustrated
parent, wondering why your life is out of control and where all
your personal space went. Your "old normal" simply needs to be
reprogrammed to the "new normal," then you can settle into the
daily rhythms of a parent's life with grace and strength.

So much of parenting is a mind game.
Just as you master parenting little tykes, they grow into
elementary age kids and you have a different set of daily
patterns and challenges. Parenting is changing you forever and
this change is for the better. Each member of a family impacts the
others. We change the tribe and the tribe changes us. If you will
let go of your other dreams and loyalties and put all your heart
and mind into building your family, you will discover the true
riches of life's most lasting treasure.

CHAPTER ONE
INTENTIONAL LIVING

Let's start by honoring something right here: you are a good parent and you are fully qualified and capable to raise a happy, confident, creative, and cooperative kid. Let's go further than that. You are already making the right decisions, not just because you're holding this book in your hands, but because the fact that you are, shows that you want to "parent on purpose" rather than by accident. That's what intentional living is about. Musing to ourselves or talking with our spouses saying, "I really hope our kids turn out OK" is not going to change a thing. Our children will turn out to be powerful, well-balanced, confident adults if we take clear steps now to make it happen. Action changes things, not thinking about it.

Many people avoid having children out of a fear that they will lose the quality of life they have found as a single person or as a couple. We assure you that you can have an awesome life and still have a family. That sounds so selfish that I can't believe I wrote it. I'd like to be more accurate and speak out of our experience as a couple. Not only did we miss nothing because of having six kids but our experience of life was exponentially deepened precisely because of the impact of our children upon our own lives. They enriched it in every way and didn't hold us back from anything.

When I proposed to Sherry I didn't have $200 in the bank. My uncle gave me the money I used to buy the ring. I took her down to the banks of a snowy river and said to her, "Marry me and I will show you the world." I didn't plan to say that. It just came out. What I had in mind was a trip to Europe for our 25th anniversary. Something about the idea of "seeing the world" kept growing in me, however. Like most young couples, we were broke financially for the first five years of our marriage. By then, we already had two kids. We had no money, but what we learned to do was to make the ultimate celebration out of every day, regardless. One of our friends called it, "doing the Quinley."

It meant packing lots of picnics and stopping almost every day to drink tea and watch the sunset. We learned that you can dress up and go to the lobbies of the world's most expensive hotels and have coffee together for an hour even if you can't afford the price of a sandwich there. There's a whole world out there waiting for you to find a way to get to it whether you have loads of money or not, and whether you have kids or not. In the end, we really did see the world, much of it anyway.

It's all about intentionality. You can get the life you want if you are willing to do what you have to do in order to get it. It's not about having enough money. It's about wanting things so badly that you make them happen, money or not. Anywhere you can go your kids can go too. They are only a hindrance to your movement if you decide to think of it that way.

If we could drill one huge pillar of foundational thought into your soul from the start of this book it would be this: your life gets simple and gains momentum when you live with intent. Make all your choices intentionally. Rule your own life and make it go in the direction it should go. You will have obstacles, surely. You may have to modify systems every few years and even renegotiate the details as you and your children grow older and have different needs, but take control of your world. Bring order to the part of creation that belongs to you.

Why it Works

Intentionality unlocks all of life's good stuff simply because we are not animals. Animals are governed by instincts which are bound up in their DNA. These urges tell them when to migrate, when to kill and when to have sex. Lemmings, those small arctic rodents, blindly follow their instincts when their numbers become too many. Without hesitation they move as a group to the edge of cliffs and jump off into the sea together. Because they are animals, they just follow these impulses, though many die from the fall or drown in the sea. Thank God, we live above the animal level.

We are humans made in the image of God Himself (Ge.1.27). Unlike animals we have an amazing power that controls our life's destiny. It's an ability called "the will." This superpower allows us to do the godlike. We can imagine ourselves outside the present circumstances of the life we are in and create, in our mind, a desired future that does not yet exist. Using that "vision" as our blueprint, we can then use our will to take charge of all the things under our control until they bring us to the imagined, preferred future and it becomes real.

We can decide to change our career, our level of fitness, obtain new skills or completely re-do our family life. Because we have the power of the will, we can make it happen. We can imagine ourselves living on the other side of our country and make it come to pass through intentionally taking charge of our actions. We are the only members of creation that have been granted this privilege of imagining a future thing, then organizing present things to bring it to pass.

Our daughter, Kristin, sat at the computer in our Thailand home one day and Googled, "best cities in America to live without a car." Portland was in the top ten so she bought a ticket and moved there with a duffle bag, knowing no one. First, she stayed with a family we met through a friend until she found a job and an apartment. (Thanks, Jeff & Liz Martin, we owe you!) Along the way she met Jason Anderson and they'll be married by the time this book is released. Kristin gets it. The only limitation we have lies inside our own minds.

In the words of Bob Marley, "Emancipate yourself from mental slavery. None but ourselves can free our minds." Throw off those shackles and build the kind of life for which you were created! You and I don't have to live in debt, with poor health or with a dysfunctional family. We can rule our own lives and bring them into line with God's dream for us.

As a human being, made in the image of our Creator God, there is very little that we cannot do if we commit to it and are willing to put all our action behind it. This is the privilege of all His children. We can all take charge of the things that are under our control and do with them what we want.

Believing this and acting upon it will change your experience of life forever. It means that you can be fit. Your family can be happy and healthy. Your children can be respectful, hardworking and grateful for the life they have received. Your marriage can be bathed with love and respect. It's a matter of living intentionally and using the power of the will. Let me give you some more examples of how this power has been put to work in our family life.

Muay Thai

As I write this, our youngest daughter, Julia, has dropped ballet and is preparing instead for her first Muay Thai (martial arts) competition bout. She can conceive of herself standing in the ring three weeks from now. There is much that she does not know as a new student of the discipline, so she uses her will to marshall her use of time (five hours of training each day), her use of money (trainers charge a fee) and her control over her own body (telling it to get up before six every day and to kick the heavy bags even though she has painful bruises already). She has always wanted to study kick boxing and now her will is making a long time dream come to pass. In three weeks her mental image of being in the ring will materialize into a real life event and she will experience what she has caused to happen. She will have created her future experience by the power of her will. Intentionality! What an amazing gift from God! Intentionality works in other, more important, areas of life as well.

Sexual Faithfulness

In many cultures fifty percent of married partners break their vow to be faithful. I intend to end my days on earth as a faithful man and I want our children to follow me in this higher path. Using my imagination, I can see myself on my deathbed, looking into my children's eyes, and saying to them all, "I promised to be faithful to your mother when I was 22 years old and now I declare to all that I have never touched another woman. I kept my promise to her, and I hold you to keep your vows also."

There's no need for me to hope that day happens for me. I have to intend to create it. If I order my actions in "the now" it will lead me to that ending one day. I need to set policies that keep me out of harm's way. I need to recognize the early impulses of sexual attraction and move quickly to escape its pull, while I have my wits about me. If I use my will and determine my actions, I will inherit my envisioned future.

We can assume that our good God will give us all the power and grace we will need. He would not have given us this amazing gift of the will unless He intended to work with us, as we will to do what is good and create our little worlds just as He created the larger world around us.

We Intend to Have Children Who Are Whole

While on the subject of sexual purity, let's add that Sherry and I intended to raise children who had their virginity intact when they left our home to go to college. We hoped that they would continue that commitment once they were on their own, but while they were in our home at least there were some clear steps we could take as parents to help secure their future as virgins when they eventually reached their 18th birthday.

We knew, statistically, that the practice of allowing them to have private contact with the opposite sex (ie., dating) at the age of 14 pretty much insured that they would have sex by age 16, so we weren't going to let that happen. To us, teens coupling up was simply a crazy, modern practice that has left millions of young people with emotional scars for life. When it's time to marry, then great, go find a marriage partner, but teens don't need to go through a series of pretend marriages and divorces to prepare them for a solid marriage in their adult lives.

If we intended to keep our kids from dating as teens, we had to start getting them on board with that idea from the time they were six years old. We also needed to help them build a solid self-identity so they wouldn't seek the validation that comes from opposite-sex romances when they were teens. We had to convince them of the damage early dating caused. It didn't take much work. They knew so many more secrets than we would ever find out about their friends' lives.

To sell this "virginal dream" to them, our kids had to come to believe in their own big future by age 13. They themselves had to perceive the impact of sexual choices on their personal destiny. The intention to land them as 18-year-old virgins drove all of our decisions concerning their personal liberty around the opposite sex until that day. By God's grace we were able to see this earnest dream fulfilled for our children and we feel they are much healthier for it.

AN EXERCISE

The point we're making in all of this is that the only way to master the things that matter in life is to have a vision in your mind, a preferred future. Let's do a mental exercise to help you put this vision into words. (You might be tempted to skip this exercise and just read on, but we really hope you won't). Grab a cup of tea. Get a notebook. Settle your mind. Take a few deep breaths and try to describe in two or three paragraphs the kind of family you want yours to be (your dream of it, not just goals or things to do). Write down how you want people to describe the character and spirit of your life and that of your family. Do this powerful exercise alone, then as a couple, and finally, as a family. When you are done, compile and craft your master vision for your family. Write it up nicely and put it in an important place, re-reading it on your anniversary or on New Year's Eve each year. Commit to it as a family. This becomes your family credo.

You can have a satisfying marriage and a refreshingly loving and transparent family. Just commit to it with all your heart as your life's highest priority, and then do the things you have to do so you can have the outcome you are dreaming of.

CHAPTER TWO
PARENTING IS NOT FAIR

Parenting is not fair. There, we said it. In order to be a consistent parent through good days and bad we found that we had to accept this fact completely and without complaining.

Here's what we mean by that. Parenting is not an equal relationship among peers. Your children will never love you the way you love them. They might not sacrifice for you at the same level that you will sacrifice for them. They will probably never express gratitude that equals the gift you give them daily over the course of their lives. This has always been true and your own parents had to deal with the same thing.

As your children get older they will not want to be with you at the same level you may want to be with them. Even worse, it is quite possible that they will remember their childhood differently than you will. For example, they may totally forget the fifty times you imperiled your career by leaving early and fighting traffic to get to their recitals and sports events. They will remember with painful clarity the one time you did not come and they scored the winning goal and looked to the stands and you weren't there. Maybe in their memory they will decide that you were hardly there at all. Parenting is not fair.

Holding your spirit in check five hundred times with a snarling, pouty, selfish teen day after day for two years will be forgotten. They will, however, remember the day that you lost it and screamed at them, forgetting entirely that the trigger was that thing they called you under their breath.

You will do your best to make every day special for them, using up twenty of your very best years and, yet, you will hear complaints and comments regardless of your efforts. You will not be able to participate fully in so many of your family's most enjoyable moments because of having to do the work required to pull off the event itself. Your kids may recall it as you always being too busy to have fun with them. Parenting is not fair.

Kids think that parents are a mountain of granite that cannot be hurt. They will never know the pain they have caused you through their words or their indifference. They will not judge things objectively and will be oh so certain that they could do things better if they were in charge.

They will seldom stop to consider what you are going through. Most of the time, it will never occur to them that you might be having a bad day yourself. Their mind may never grasp the possibility that when they were sick and feeling so miserable, you might have been just as sick yourself, yet you took care of them.

This myopia is particularly true when they reach their teens and become obsessed with fitting in and being approved by their peers (most of whom they'll hardly know after graduating high school). When you restrain them from going out because you noticed the text message on their phone revealing the "real plan" for the night you'll catch Hell from them, just for trying to keep Hell away from them. Kids never understand how much work they were to raise.

Hopefully, you will also have sweet stories of the times when your children were extra thoughtful of you. Some kids are amazingly considerate. Ours certainly were, but we had our moments of frustration with most of them also.

Even if your kids are angels, parenting is still not fair. These kids you love so much are in the process of leaving you behind with every passing day, even as you watch over them earnestly and render loving care. You job is to sacrifice for them so they can have a better life. They will never understand how much it cost you to be their parent.

Parenthood is not Just Friendship

Parenting is not a friendship. Your kids have access to hundreds of friends. They only have one set of parents, though. Nobody, and I mean nobody, holds the unique legal, spiritual and relational position that you do as their parent. God used your body to create them. God Himself has entrusted you with total custody of their life until you (not the government) determine that they are competent to stand alone and gradually release them to adulthood.

Remember also that friendships exist for the period in which it meets the needs of both parties. When you move on in life, you reach out for new friends who share a life more similar to the way yours is developing. Friendships come and go. Parents are parents forever. Your kids need a parent more than they need another buddy.

Friends bare their soul and pour out their inner hurts to each other. Thinking about sharing all the pain in your heart with your kids? Please don't. Frustrated with your marriage partner? Keep it to yourself. Your children need at least one stable adult they can lash their boat to in stormy seas, and you need to be that person. All adults are struggling to deal with a certain amount of personal pain inside, from the vestiges of our childhood traumas, from broken adult relationships or simply from living in a messed up world. These are our personal issues. Some of them are known and open, and we do well to be honest about them with everyone who lives with us. Our heaviest burdens, however, need to be shared with our adult friends or with our spouse. Please don't lay all your unprocessed stuff on your kids. Your relationship toward them isn't just another friendship. It's parenthood. It's about them, not you.

People your kids think of fondly as uncles and aunts may actually be true sources of trouble for you. Unloading this on your kids unnecessarily removes one more pillar of their security. They will wonder if anyone is good. Couples in ministry, please don't share with your kids the painful realities going on in the church, or paint a member as attacking you. Your children may have loved that person before, and now they will come to mistrust the church that you actually love so much, despite the hassles that come from serving it.

Their minds can't process the things you are dealing with. They have true issues of their own that come from their experiences in school and with friends. Don't add adult-sized issues to their childhood load. Single moms, try not to turn your responsible daughters into your personal caregivers. You may need help to survive life, but they also need the few relatively carefree years in their later teens before the heaviness of adult life rests on their shoulders permanently.

Parenting is a Mission

Parenting is a mission, a holy calling. Like the child of Zecharias and Elizabeth, (Lk. 1.13ff.) your child has been born with a divine destiny to fulfill. They have been given a unique gift-mix and special circumstances to help shape them. Fulfilling their life's mission is their own burden. Preparing them to face it successfully is yours.

They will face some truly backbreaking challenges along their quest, just as you have. They will be wounded in the battle of life and will have to face their own inner demons and an evil world system that will grow ever more powerful by the time they are adults. They need to be equipped for their mission and you are the one called to impart this to them. Your relationship with your kids is not a fair and equal one that meets all your personal needs as you work to meet theirs too. It is completely one-sided. It will never be "fair" and if you can just accept that and not expect them to "be there for you," then you will be able to deal with the demands of parenting.

CHAPTER THREE
WHAT ABOUT ME?

Someone may protest, "Who then will be my crying shoulder when I need one?" Get an adult friend. "Who will make me happy?" Meet your own needs. Eat right. Go out and play. Enjoy music and get a life of your own. Take dance lessons. Develop your own spiritual core and give yourself completely to one huge lifetime love with your partner.

Sherry and I live in the developing world where some parents ask, "Who is going to look out for my retirement money then?" You are. You're the grown up. So take care of yourself while you take care of everyone else. Nations of poverty see children as a means of constant provision for their parents. This leads to many crippling practices, even as extreme as sending kids to work in factories at ten. In many nations, kids are expected to start supporting their parents just after graduation. That means they cut their professional education short and, instead of developing a strong career path, take the first entry-level job they can find and never really move up in the world.

If you give your child a complete childhood they won't be stuck in perpetual adolescence as adults. Some children don't get to be children long enough before being saddled with the load of their parents' responsibilities. Young people need a space of time when they are simply children and the world is wonderful. Help them wrap up being a child, then coach them until they successfully navigate their teen and early adult years.

Raising Strong Children

The good news is that if you do your job of raising independent children you won't need to support your kids after their early twenties. Your peak earning years are your 50's and 60's anyway so when the nest empties in your 40's, "get your game on" business-wise for the next 30 years and prepare for your own late-life needs. Your children will certainly care for you when you really can't fend for yourself, but with today's life expectancies they will probably be approaching their 60's themselves by the time you need this help.

Children become strong when they are raised by an adult who is a tower of strength and security. They live under the shelter of this parent and draw confidence from their parents' strength. They will have gained the strength that comes from having a powerful ally behind them and they will be strong for their own children as well, following your good example.

What Parenthood Does to Us

Parenting is not fair but if you will give yourself to it willingly and cheerfully each day, it will bring you to the deepest level of spiritual and emotional maturity you will ever find as a human. The daily pressures you face will build deep reserves of strong character in you.

Dying to yourself and sacrificing your personal desires will kill much of the selfishness in you and liberate you to live generously. You might not be willing to make these extreme daily sacrifices for random strangers, but when you look into the eyes of your child and see familiar elements of yourself in them, you will gladly live and die for them.

Give parenthood a decade or two to work on you, and you will, in short, become the deepest and best version of yourself. You will find yourself more in tune with the needs of others. Repeatedly sacrificing your own comfort will mature you, make you noble, and cause you to see the world outside of yourself, and that's where all the amazing things in life are to be found.

God reveals much about Himself when we become parents. I remember loving Sherry so much and how our love totally filled up all the need I had for relationship. By the time we'd been married a year, though, Sherry started talking about wanting a baby. I resisted initially, wanting it to be "just us" for a while longer, but I felt the Lord telling me to listen to her. I wondered if I had the love in me for a baby. Then Andrew popped out, his head a flame of red hair, and "father's love" exploded inside my heart toward him. I had never experienced this kind of love. I just wanted to be with Andrew every day. I was captivated by every little thing he did and was overjoyed to celebrate all his "firsts." He slept on my chest often and I looked down on him in wonder and gratefulness.

When Andrew was scarcely a year old Sherry started talking about wanting another baby and the cycle repeated itself. I seriously doubted whether I had any more love in me. I just couldn't imagine loving another child. It seemed like Andrew took it all and I didn't want another child to feel any less attachment from me. Then Kristin made her grand entrance and a tsunami of new love surged out of my deepest soul. I never had so much love before! She was magic and I immediately had twice the love, even more. The addition of every new child only deepened the flow and caused the multiplication of love within me.

Eventually we found ourselves with six children around the table. Each brought a friend home for dinner many nights. I know that sounds like disaster, but it was wonderful! We ate our meals amid the din of three simultaneous conversations, each shouted above the other. Sometimes someone would break out in song and everyone followed. Story after story kept our sides splitting from laughter. Visitors would sit in stunned silence and watch the happy chaos.

Now our kids have left the nest. Only two will be unmarried by the end of this year. They are all strong and good. We have entered our middle years with them now, celebrating their marriages, their early career moves and the joy of them receiving their own children. (Grandchildren really are so amazing. When they throw their arms open, and call your name, and come running to meet you, time stops). Watching our children parent their own children with such balance and confidence gives us strong hope for our family's future. They will go higher than we ever did in our own lifetimes.

Sherry and I are satisfied with our lives. If we died now, we'd die fulfilled. Mostly it's because of our children. Raising them to be healthy and strong was the most important thing we ever accomplished. We can be a friend to many, but a parent to only a few. Only a parent gets to experience all these joys. It's true, "parenting is not fair." We get the best end of the deal.

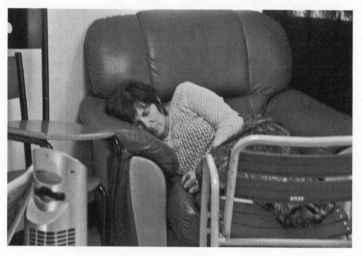

Parenting is pretty tiring work but it's worth it!

CHAPTER FOUR
NAMING YOUR CHILDREN

One of the first things we do as parents when we learn that we are expecting is to begin trying to pick out a name for our child. Some people coordinate the names of all their kids in cute ways or make them all start with the same letter. We met dozens of Filipinos with the names, Boy and Girlie, often because nobody filled in the birth papers at the hospital so the standard "(Boy) Garcia" became their legal name. It happens in other countries as well. I read of someone in India who had no personal name beyond "Boy." His family just never named him. His first grade teacher needed something to write in the class ledger and so gave him the name of a Hindu god, which became his name for life.

Thai parents sometimes give playful names to their kids. We know more than one girl named "Ice Cream" and know others with names like "Postage Stamp" and siblings named "Light" and "Switch." Two of our best friends are named "Bear" and "Tree." Some particularly beautiful children in tribal societies are given names like "Ugly" so the demons won't be jealous and harm them. Heavyweight boxer, George Foreman, kept things simple. He has five sons. All are named George Foreman. While modern people may choose names frivolously, for most of the history of the world naming children was a solemn and serious business.

Names Have Spiritual Power

In the ancient world, as in the Bible, it was believed that a person's name held a certain power over them. It was a revelation of the child's character, a vision for how they would be as a person or even a prophecy about the life they would lead. This label would stick to the child and they would hear it all of their lives, which helped them prepare their minds to fulfill the destiny prophesied over them by their parents. The name had the power in itself to bring to pass what was spoken over the child.

This isn't just superstition. It's how God sees things. The power to name a thing is lordship over it and has an impact on its destiny. Read the creation story in Genesis. It describes how God created our world, item by item, just by calling their names out. God named humans, "man." It meant that, unlike all the other animals, we had been made in the divine nature of God, Himself. He names the first man, "Adam" (man from the red earth) and then gives him the privilege of naming all the animals and, consequently, of ruling over them.

Many times in the Bible when a child of special destiny was to be born, God intercepted the parents with an angel before they could attach the wrong name to the child. He told them what the child's proper name must be. The forerunner of the Messiah had to be named, "John" (Jehovah is showing grace and mercy) because that's what John's life was all about. He intercepted people who were heading for certain judgment and destruction and told them that God was extending forgiveness to them if they would just stop their sinning and turn around. The incarnated child of God through Mary had to be named, "Jesus" (Savior), because the purpose of His life would be to save us and the rest of creation and bring us safely into God's Kingdom forever.

Names matter.

Names are the foundation of our identity. A female friend from India told us that when a woman in her caste marries, she loses all of her names and becomes an entirely new person name-wise. She said that she and her new husband thought long and hard about her new name. When Hindu or Buddhists become Christians they or their pastor typically choose a name from the Bible, and they go by that name from the day of their baptism.

Nicknames and Labels

Maybe nicknames say more about us than our formal names. Such names have a warm history and are generally given by someone who knows us well. In the military or other high-value membership cultures, you really aren't in the group until someone chooses a nickname for you. These names usually come from a story about your role or experience in the group, something that was noticed to be different about you.

Some names, on the other hand, come from school bullies and are used to taunt and humiliate us. It's not uncommon to hear an adult tell the story of how a major part of their life's choices have been related to a name they were called in school. It either crushed their spirit or put such a determination in them to "show them wrong" that they blossomed from an ugly duckling to a graceful swan.

Names matter.

Labeling Our Children

We're talking about identity formation, our core understanding of who we are. We define children in so many ways. The first label occurs within seconds of a birth when everyone looks for genitals and someone cries out with joy, "It's a girl!" or, "It's a boy!" Our ideas about gender roles are applied to them.

Then we decide who they look like and start repeating that, attaching their identity in part to a life lived by another person. After that, we notice their personal characteristics, strengths and weaknesses and start forming an opinion of these and speak them out. Children receive much of their identity in this way.

The most common form of naming we do in creating our child's personal identity comes through things we say to them. Any time we begin a sentence with, "You are so…," we need to think carefully about the words we will use to finish that sentence. "You are so stubborn!" sticks to them and pretty much insures additional stubbornness to come.

Think of the impact of hearing even something like, "You are just like your father!" Hopefully, you are saying that the child's father is a hero to you and you are so glad they are like him but, perhaps, you have actually made two statements in one. First, you don't like their father in some way and, second, that this same characteristic is in them too and you don't like them for the same reason.

Just open your ears for a week and record all the things you hear parents say to their children about who they are. Hopefully, you will hear a symphony of positivity, but the odds are you will become aware of how much negative labeling many kids endure. The more dysfunctional the family, the more negative their words. We actually had a mother introduce us to her kids, and in the presence of them all, tell us which one was her favorite and which one was the smartest, as though creating rivalry among them was her intention.

It's a good starting place to listen to the words other parents pour out, but more important is the habit of listening to the words that are coming out of our own mouths. Listen to your own words when you are tense with them. Pay attention to what you say about them. We hope you will be pleasantly surprised by how much grace seasons your speech. If not, then you need to take charge of your speaking ability and make it work for good. Blessed is the child who has parents who see the wondrous things inside and call them out through their words.

Naming Your Child to Others

The only thing more powerful than words spoken directly to a child are words spoken about the child to others while the child is present. Introducing your child to others is always a golden opportunity. As young parents, Sherry and I were eager to show that we were doing a good job. In a bookstore we ran into an older gentleman we admired. Sherry told our four-year-old son to greet the stranger and the child shied away a bit. Embarrassed, Sherry replied apologetically, "He's just shy."

That's when we got a major parenting lesson. The gentleman had a strong fatherly grace about him so we didn't chafe as he kindly replied, "And does he really need to hear you say that about him?" In one moment we recognized that our child would probably never forget anything he heard us say to others about him. We were so grateful for this correction while we were still young parents.

Parents are sinners too and we all have to guard against letting the darkness inside of us come out and wound our children. This is even more the case in a family torn by divorce. It's almost automatic to place the child in the middle of the frustrations being experienced by both adults. Guard your words, dear friend. They have a power greater than you know.

CHAPTER FIVE
LIFE & DEATH IS
IN THE TONGUE

What if your spoken words as parents had the power to create the thing you said? What if, by saying to a child, "You are so musical," you could release the gift of music inside them? What if, by saying to others out loud, "David is so loving!", David truly became so? Would you use that power more if you believed in it?

God says it is so. "Death and life are in the power of the tongue: and they that love it shall eat the fruit thereof" (Proverbs 18.21 KJV). Call it self-fulfilling prophesies, or call it the living spiritual power contained in our words, or call it psychology but whenever we speak into the life of another person something good or bad will happen as a result.

The Bible says that our words can bring death: death to self-worth, death to confidence, and death to a positive life vision. We have occasionally watched, with anguished wonder, the slow erosion of strong men under the daily dripping of acid from the lips of their wives. Though these men were physically strong, their courage steadily dissolved over the course of living for a decade under the ceaseless negativity behind the words of their 100-pound wives. In time, their giant shoulders began to slump and their spirit became crushed just by the lack of confidence their wife had in them and by the way she caused them to redefine themselves as "a disappointment" through her words. It is a horrible thing to observe. Words have such power to destroy.

Thank God, there is life in the tongue too! We've also been present during the healing of countless wounded souls. These found their wholeness simply because they met a new person who understood how to speak life, and who brought them into a new, positive friendship circle. Here, they heard thousands of words of love, vision and encouragement. These living words swirled all around them, then moved inside their conscious minds and they began to hope again. This is what it means to "minister" to someone. God will give all of us countless opportunities to unlock the potential of others through releasing our anointed words into them.

You can always spot a child who has been raised by parents who understand the power of life that is in the tongue. It doesn't work by simply flattering your always "special" child but by really looking into them and studying them like a science, then calling out the name of every good thing you see in them with words like, "One of your superpowers is that you really listen to others. You truly see people and they can feel it. You are going to help so many people in your lifetime." Kids don't forget words like that.

What happens in an example like this? You call out something that is alive in them and they feel the truth of it. When people hear the truth they recognize it. You put a name on a swirling thing in their soul, and through calling it by name, you bring it into the real world. That's the power of naming. If Sherry and I have any fruit from our years of ministry it comes primarily from honoring and confidently using this great gift from God in the lives of others. We all have a mouth. We just need to learn to use it for something besides eating.

Once a parent can comprehend the power of their words in the life of their child, they can begin using it intentionally to build their children up each day.

Naming Street Kids

The most powerful example of naming children we've seen comes from the street ministry of Joann Luciano in Metro Manila. Each week Joann and her team of 100 young people take to the streets in some of the toughest neighborhoods in Manila. I'm not sure I can adequately describe this level of poverty. Millions of children in Manila are raised just over the walls from large industrial or commercial sections of the city. Their families build flimsy housing from whatever they find at hand, usually aluminum sheets and a few boards. Their floors are often clay. These shanties are nested like beehives along the railways and canals situated on the small strips of land reserved by the government as a right-of-way.

Industrial run-off mixes with the sewage from tens of thousands of these families. This toxic sludge runs in open ditches until it empties into their streams and canals. There is no garbage pickup so everyone throws their garbage in the canals too. When the tropical heat gets too oppressive, the kids play games and jump off the railroad trestles into this septic pool to cool off. Men sit gambling from morning till night, while women feed the chickens that roam freely and then squat by basins all day long washing clothes by hand to try and earn enough money just to buy a daily meal for the family.

Into this place of hopelessness Joann Luciano goes every weekend, armed with a sparkling attitude, a bunch of songs, some crackers, powdered juice drinks and the Gospel. She and her team move from barrio to barrio, gathering children in groups of 70. The kids sit in disciplined rows and pay attention to every word that comes out of the mouth of Joann and her team. By the end of each weekend, Joann's team has had face-to-face interactions with 9,000 children.

Her message is simple and powerful. "God has a plan to save you and your entire family and to take you out of this place. His plan is you. He is going to change you from the inside out through the power of the blood of Jesus. Then he is going to start using you to bless others. You are the child of promise in your family. You are going to lead them to God, and you will also be the one to lead them out of this place one day. If you will live a truly Christian life, work hard on your grades and be faithful in the Sidewalk Sunday School ministry, we will train you to become one of our leaders. Serve faithfully as a leader and we will make sure you go to college too. You are going to change your family's story."

Many of the kids hearing this have already grown accustomed to being routinely beaten or sexually-abused. All of them have lice and worms. Some have festering wounds on their legs from the sewage they wade through when it rains, but in their eyes a candle starts to flicker and the light grows brighter every week as she fuels it with her confident declarations. On weekends they learn the songs and they study God's word to find the truth about His plans for them. Then on Monday, they will comb their hair and join the other "Sidewalk Kids" as they march off to school, determined to succeed. Joann has shown them a new path of life and a new name to live up to, "Overcomer." (If you would like to sponsor one of Joann's kids just visit the www.emergemissions.org website.)

Renaming

Sometimes the biggest thing holding a person back is simply a negative self-identity. They see themselves as weak, powerless, damaged or handicapped in some way. These people need to be "rebranded." They need someone with authority over them to give them a new name and call them a new thing so they can be recreated and live another life.

Jesus chose a fisherman named Simon and trained him to be his right-hand-man. Simon was big and boisterous, but also weak and fearful of the opinions of others. Jesus felt that part of his problem was in his name, Simon. It meant a weak, thin reed. His father probably chose it because in Israel's past a famous man had worn that name. Sometimes a person's big noisy presence and loud attitudes are really a cover-up for their deep sense of insecurity. This was certainly the case with Simon.

In John 1.42 Jesus tells Simon that he's changing his name. He says, "Your new name is the Rock." Rocky! What an awesome upgrading of his name and self-image! I can't imagine how it must have felt to hear your new, future-shaping name as it rolled off the lips of Jesus for the first time.

God made the world by calling it out with names. He changed futures by changing names throughout history and He's not finished yet. He changed the names of Abraham and Sarah and made a covenant with them. He changed the name of Jacob (deceiver) to Israel (one who prevails with God). Removing negative labels and replacing them with well-chosen names is part of the process of transformation. The new name had power to create the thought behind it. The heart of the Gospel is the promise of change. He can change you and He can teach you how to bring change to others.

I don't know what labels you carry. I hope they are powerful and life-giving, but for most of us there is real and present damage from life-sucking ideas that are stuck in our head. God wants to set you free from anything that is wounded in your self image. You hold the keys to your own mind and it will fall to you to reject and replace the negative labels you might be carrying. Just know that these labels are lies. The only one who knows the truth about you is the One who made you and He looks at you in love.

Maybe you have earned your bad labels through mistakes in your past. Good news again! He is God of the Second Chance. Be honest with God, yourself and others about the mistakes you have made, then brush off the dirt of falling down and get back in the race. There is nothing God won't forgive and there is no one beyond His help if they will cry out and ask for it.

Your Ministry of Renaming Others

Sometimes a person gets stuck in a bad situation and they need a fresh start. As adults with naming power let's use it to remove old labels from children and stop referring to the mistakes of their past. See them as people who are positively evolving and learning from past mistakes.

This is particularly important with teens who get off track and lose their way. It's easy to become, stuck with a label like "the dope head," "the coward," "that girl who got pregnant," or "the loser." People struggling against inner failure need some reason to hope. It would be great if all your mistakes could be erased each night as you slept and you really did get to make a fresh start. It would be even better, if people with power would actively rip our old labels off of us and replace them with something positive.

When I was in middle school there was this girl who was sort of pretty but very quiet. I don't know why, because there was nothing wrong with her, but she was never included in any group. She didn't look sad, only awkward. Every day held the same for her. Nobody was going to talk with her and she would eat alone. Then one day I saw her sitting on the steps with one of the main jocks in the school. Her face was beaming. She was her natural self and wasn't throwing herself at him, but you could tell that she really appreciated someone so popular taking the time to talk with her. It started being a daily thing, and within a week she was on the "A" list for the rest of her career in school. All it took was one person to name her, "desirable" and the world read the sign and acted accordingly. Even our young children have the power to redirect the futures of others through their including unpopular kids and by removing hurtful names and replacing them with positive nicknames like Jesus did.

Our Final Name

Throughout our life we will wear many titles and be called by many names. Our grandson, August, calls Sherry, "Sherbear." Most of our Medialight students call her, "Mom." When we moved to Thailand I learned that Chuck, in Thai, means "to have a convulsion," so here I became "Chahlee." In the academic world, I'm "Dr. Quinley." At the church I was "Pastor Chuck." Our names and titles change with our circumstances. Strangely, all our names are given to us by others. They got their names from others as well.

One, day, when our earthly life is concluded, we will be weighed by our Creator. On that day, if we have proven to be overcomers, we will be given the ultimate name that summarizes all that we are as a person.

**"And I will give him a white stone, and on the stone a new name written which no one knows except him who receives it."
Rev. 2.17 NKJV.**

This is the name for us that is known only by God Himself. More than anything we have ever been called, this name suits us perfectly. It will summarize the essence of our lives, lived under His love and grace. He will reveal it to us privately, because only the two of us know what we've been through together in all the tests and trials of earthly life. It will be the highest validation we could ever receive, the honoring of our lifetime effort to live as a light in the world. The goal of every believing family should be to prepare ourselves and others for this day. If we have allowed our life as a family on a mission to do it's proper work within us, then this will be a happy day for all of us.

CHAPTER SIX
THE ULTIMATE TEST OF PARENTING

Early in our marriage I was away on a trip and was invited into a Hispanic family's home for dinner. Their two older children joined us at the table, along with a friend they had brought along with them. We enjoyed our delicious, home-cooked meal and a happy conversation. After the meal, the kids helped clear the table and returned to set up coffee and dessert.

At this point, the conversation went deeper and the mother began steering it into more personal matters. I wondered if I was intruding and thought it might be uncomfortable for the young college students, but to my surprise they began to openly talk about their insecurities, struggles and sins. The dad was wise, the mother kind and loving, and I watched in rapt wonder, observing the flow of the Holy Spirit between everyone at the table. Soon, I became an equal part of the conversation. We all became so honest and unguarded in each other's presence, certain of our acceptance. We were humans on our own unique path of life and we needed this time to be honest. We needed and received each other's support so we could all be healed. We prayed together, the parents laying their hands on their children and their friend.

I tried to sleep that night but I had been taken by the vision of what I had witnessed. I couldn't wait to get back to Sherry and unpack the lessons from this night. This became our goal as parents—that our children would tell us the truth about their lives through all the stages in their development.

If we had the access to their heart to ask hard questions, and if they felt the security to honestly answer us then we would know that we had a true bond with our children. To obtain such trust, we had to start young and not allow their teenage growth to cause a gap to form between us.

The Best Hour of the Day

With six kids, Sherry and I knew that it would be easy to miss giving one of them the attention they needed. Middle children, in particular, will allow their needs to be overlooked if parents aren't careful to focus on them. If we wanted a tightly bonded family we needed time to touch and have extended conversations with each child. We developed a habit where the last thing we did at the end of every day was to crawl into the bed of each child. There we would hold them in the darkness and talk for a while.

We had a house full of kids, remember, so it took an entire hour each night to complete this ritual. Sherry and I went in different directions and spent ten minutes with each child. If one fell asleep we would move on, ending with the older kids who generally had more to talk out in the quiet darkness. It proved to be the best hour of every day and we got to know more about our children than we could have ever known otherwise. Kids will tell you things in the darkness they will never have the courage to say in the daylight.

Growing up
in an eclectic
mix of color
and language
has made our
kids colorblind,
thank God.

Honest, Non-judgmental Family Culture

Whatever it took, we were determined to keep the channels of communication working between all of us. Our family had to feel safe. The atmosphere needed to be encouraging and accepting, free from judgment. In order to have this we needed to welcome some alternative people into our lives and love them whether they ever came close to having the beliefs and values we cherished. We welcomed strangers of many kinds into our home for a meal or to sleep over for a few days. We embraced them as persons the best we could and added them to our growing collection of amazing friends. Honestly, it's a delicate thing to be both the confidant for your child and the one who can put them on restriction. The wonderful Hispanic family did it, however, so we knew we could do it too.

SECTION TWO
Learning to Show True Love

Families are built on love and loyalty.

This section focuses on describing the specific kind of love a healthy family needs. We also turn our attention to some ideas for teaching children how to love openly, for making yours a family that shows love to outsiders, and for making certain that the bond of love between husband and wife is not neglected by an exclusive focus on raising children.

CHAPTER SEVEN
RISING ABOVE PERFORMANCE-BASED ACCEPTANCE

We were visiting with some university students recently when the subject of faith came up. The young lady I was speaking with said, "I am Buddhist, but I am very interested in learning more about Jesu (Jesus)." I asked her why and she said, "His is the religion of love and I want to know about real love." Wow! We were so glad she had had such a warm experience with the followers of Jesus that she saw Christianity in this light.

I asked, "What do you know about the teachings of Jesus?" to which she replied confidently, "I know that we must do good things and that those things will make God love us!" "Oh," I said, "that's not it at all. The Bible says that even when we were at our most evil and had done our worst things, God already loved us. He will not stop loving us, because His inner nature is Love." She sat stunned at the big thought of God's "agape" kind of love, and finally replied, "I learned a lot today."

God's love is so different from ours. Most human love isn't really love at all. It's what we might call, "performance-based acceptance." It's the very human kind of love the Chinese student was referring to. We are loved by others because we are good to them. We are honored because we win. Many children only receive their family's approval when they earn it.

Even if you excel at sports, academics, beauty or by making money, it's never enough. You might have been the champion last year, but no one can remain champion forever. Every success only makes the hurdles higher next time. Perfect performance is simply not sustainable. That's why stars and champions often feel insecure despite having a wall filled with trophies. Once this need to earn love has been ingrained in a child, they may never be able to get off the approval-seeking treadmill. They may never truly live a life of their own.

Kristin Excels

When she was four, we put Kristin in what they called in Manila, "Kinder-prep." We figured she'd color and play and sing. We soon found out that prep was serious business. There were exams and grade point averages and tips on "how to accelerate your child's learning." We were talking to a mother who had a child in a competing school. She said that her son would be with a tutor for the next week, studying for his finals. "Finals?!" we exclaimed, "He's only four!" "But only the top ten percent can go into the executive program," came the reply.

We didn't bother telling Kristin that she should be stressed out about her grades. She was learning all that she needed to learn at age four and we had no doubt about her intelligence and overall ability. In fact, we could already see one of her superpowers glimmering within her. The award she received at graduation that year only confirmed it. At the ceremony where she passed from "prep" into full kindergarten, the headmaster called out her name to receive a notable award, "Friendliest!" Yep, that's Kristin! She's never met a stranger. We knew that her bold friendliness was the ability that would open doors for her throughout her lifetime. She was beaming at her award and so were we.

We feel that a parent should keep their focus on what kind of person their child is, not on what they have done to make them proud in areas where humans most often compete (sports, academics, appearance, etc.). Who we are is more important than what we do. Being recognized for who we are rather than for our performance forms the ground for a more secure identity.

There is little need to stress out your diligent child regarding their low math grade. When was the last time anyone asked what you scored on your history exam? These are passing matters. The deeper issue is whether they have solid character and whether they know their gifts and are learning to use them effectively. The cream always rises to the top eventually. You cannot keep quality people down. The excellence of their inner foundation causes them to catch the eye of their employers and advancement follows. The quality of their secure character gives them the staying power to outlast their rivals in the ceaseless competition of life.

Who Are You?

Remove the labels from us and who are we? If I ask someone who they are they might say, "Janice Thompson." No, that's just your name and you didn't even choose it. Who are you? "I'm a florist." No, that's what you do for a job. Your job will change many times in your life. Who are you? "I'm a wife and a mother." Those are two of your roles, etc. Who are you? That is the question that eats at us. It's the fuel that drives us to establish a sense of identity for ourselves. For someone who grew up under adults that gave only performance-based acceptance, seeking a solid sense of personal identity becomes a lifetime quest.

How many men and women live with crippling insecurities all because they received performance-based acceptance throughout their earliest years? Performance-based is bad enough, but some kids receive only appearance-based acceptance. They have to be beautiful enough in public to make their parents feel like stars themselves. Makeup on 8-year-olds? We've all seen it.

"The Showcase Family"

We all face the normal social pressure that comes from membership in any close community, whether it's family or the strata of society you come from. "What will our neighbors say?" "What will people think?" These cries of fearful insecurity have often been uttered by parents around the world from the dawn of civilization.

Some careers battle this more than others. One of the additional pressures that goes with public leadership is having your private world brought under scrutiny because of your professional world. Does my plumber have orderly children? What is the state of his marriage? Who knows? Why even ask? It has nothing to do with why I call him if my pipes get clogged. In high-profile leadership, celebrity life, or politics this is an entirely different matter because of the pressure to live an exemplary life.

This gives rise to one of the most damaged forms of family, the "Showcase Family." The showcase family isn't real. It's a play, put on to deceive others into believing that this family is a perfect family, compliant with all required norms and expectations. In order to keep up the illusion, the children must be recruited into the cause and taught to play an act around other people as well. Think about how this training affects a child. Children are embarrassingly honest. It's their childlike nature. Into their world comes this adult, someone they trust and love, and routinely trains them to become fake in front of others so the family can keep up appearances.

The fraud of a showcase family comes from the insecurity of the parents. They are afraid of being judged by others and are unwilling to admit that their family is human and flawed, like all the other families in the world. Perpetuating the showcase myth saps all the energy you need for building a real family. If you were raised in a family like this you will automatically follow this pattern in your own home one day. If we believe ourselves to be somehow inferior to others it will affect the way we shape our children. Without meaning to, we will sow seeds of insecurity in their tender hearts.

Agape-level Acceptance

The ancient Greeks had three words to describe love. They had separate words that described brotherly friendship, maternal nursing, or sexual love. The love they received from Jesus didn't fit into any of these categories. Early Christians had to coin another love word, "agape." Agape is unlike all the other loves because it does not require lovability in the object. You can't earn agape love because you aren't the source of it. It comes from the heart of the Great Lover. John tells us that in the deepest part of His inner nature, "God is agape."

Here's how 1 John 4.7-9 reads with the word agape placed where it comes in the original Greek text:

"Beloved, let us agape one another, for agape comes from God. Everyone who agapes has been born of God and knows God. Whoever does not agape does not know God because God is agape. This is how God demonstrated His agape among us: He sent His one and only Son into the world that we might live through Him." (My translation.)

Here's another verse to ponder:

Romans 5.7-8 (NIV) "...For a good person someone might possibly dare to die. But God demonstrates his own (agape) love for us in this: While we were still sinners, Christ died for us." (Parenthesis mine.)

Healing Ourselves First

We can't give our children something we don't have ourselves. If you are trapped on a performance treadmill where you can only accept yourself when you are perfectly meeting your own expectations, you are not going to be able to give your precious little ones their full acceptance, regardless of their performance. If we can become liberated from doing this to ourselves, we can avoid doing it to our children as well.

Nurturing children who have a secure, guilt-free identity requires us to first receive unmerited love from God ourselves. We parents need to take God's agape love and wrap it around us like a thick mink coat on a freezing winter's day. Have you ever just reveled in the luxury of being accepted, embraced and loved unto death by God? He knows the truth about us. At our worst, we are sinners and rebels against Him. At our best, our righteousness is still a filthy rag compared to His holiness. We didn't earn His love when we were living as sinners and we can't keep His love by our good works after we make peace with Him either.

He loves us because He loves. It's not because we did—or one day will do—anything special or worthy. The glory goes to God who alone loves with complete Agape. If we can convince ourselves that we are completely known and yet completely loved by our Creator it will begin to unshackle us. It may happen in layers and we might find ourselves often taking two steps forward and one step back from time to time, but that's progress! Eventually, God's love will find a home in us and we will become consciously aware of its abiding presence. We can feel accepted, dear friend. God wants that for all of us.

God's goal ultimately is that His unconditional love will fill us and then begin to flow out of us and onto others. He will teach us to love in the same way He is always loving us.

Those who love with agape are able to love their children regardless of their accomplishments or their absence of them. Becoming a dispenser of agape love should start closest to home, for that is the truest laboratory for working it out, but true agape love will refuse to be confined to your family alone. When you become a giver of unconditional acceptance, you will start to function as God's point of grace upon the earth.

CHAPTER EIGHT
BONDING BEFORE ALL ELSE

"Something's not right with this baby," Sherry told me with concern. "Andrew connected to me as soon as he was born, but watch Kristin. Have you noticed that she doesn't make eye contact with anyone, not even with me when I hold her or nurse her? She isn't bonding to people for some reason." Sherry was only 26, but she could already tune in to the impulses in the souls of her children.

We lived in Jamaica in those days, but I was also enrolled in a three-year graduate program in the States. This called for me to be apart from her and the kids for one month, twice a year.

I asked Sherry, "What can we do about it?" She replied, "For the next 30 days while you're away, I'm going to sit in that rocking chair, cuddle and talk to my baby until I can get her to come out and connect with me. That's my plan. I'm not raising a detached child." Four weeks later I returned home to a baby that smiled, cooed and made solid eye contact when anyone held her. Sherry was glowing. Kristin's bonding ability was now jump-started.

The heart of every healthy family is a bond of love that makes you support, protect and defend each other above all others. Our friend, Paul, has a scar on his belly from the surgery where he received a donated kidney. He had been slowly dying, but this huge sacrifice gave him a second life. Where did he get the kidney? His sister gave it to him.

A healthy family is a well-bonded family. Perhaps the highest compliment we ever received about our family came from an eighth-grade schoolmate of Julia's named Lydia who shared her perception of us, "Your family is like... the Cullens!" Coming from a member of the Twilight-saga generation, that was high praise. It said that she perceived our family to be a benevolent, powerful, unified force where each member was certain to be protected by the others no matter what the cost. Even though she was comparing us to a family of vampires, the idea still made me smile.

We believe that a family is the most powerful force on earth. Nothing will give you a better start in life than simply to be raised in a healthy, loving home. Even grown people can be restored and renewed just from spending a few days hanging out with a solid family. After just one day in our noisy house, a Chinese visitor once said, with deep appreciation, "I have never seen love before. Thank you."

The bond among the members of our family creates our security as a group. Without it we stand in danger of ceasing to even exist as a family. Jesus said that in the last days, "the love of many will grow cold." We were determined not to let this happen to us. Sherry and I knew that we were the beloved children of God, that we had His love inside of us, and that we could release love on others any time we wanted to. We wanted to nurture a family that knew how to express love and did it lavishly.

The First Principle

Family begins with bonding. It is the first principle in family and in ministry. Some families are better bonded than others. You can just feel the warmth the moment you enter their home. It is an upbeat, happy, welcoming place that would make anyone rush home from work or school just to be there.

In other homes, however, there seems to be no beating heart. People are scattered throughout the house. You hear the front door open and close as people come and go without a word. The TV is on the whole time. Even when people are in the same room they don't speak. They stare into their phones, texting the ones who are more important to them. In this kind of family, everyone lives under the same roof technically, but there is no unity to their existence. They aren't a family, or even a team.

The Bond Makes Control Bearable

In terms of parenting, it is the bond that makes control bearable for a child. The bond causes a healthy child to accept parental guidance, whether they are six or sixteen. They love their parents and know that their parents' control and concern is simply a reflection of their own great value and an expression of their parents' love toward them. Discipline won't work without the underpinning of a bond to support it.

The bond is what makes a rebellious child take the discipline they deserve so their path can be corrected. Even if they think they might be physically stronger than their parent, they submit because of the bond.

So many great moments around campfires.

Improving Your Family's Bond

Building a bonded family starts with the intent to do it. Since the bond is for the family's highest good, all family members need to agree that our individual freedoms must yield in favor of the greater good of the family bond. (In some marriages, frankly, one partner may just have to take the initiative alone and start working on this aspect of their family life till it catches on.)

The definitive book on bonding, as far as we are concerned, was written by Dr. Donald Joy and it is entitled, simply, <u>Bonding</u>. I was privileged to study under Dr. Joy. In college I took teachers more than courses. I knew I wanted to take Dr. Joy's classes after he set his eyes on me one day as I walked down the hallowed halls of Asbury Seminary. I remember feeling particularly overwhelmed by the workload of the intensive semester. With confidence he said, "Hey, you look like you could use a hug." Then he wrapped me up in a good bear hug and held it for a second. I didn't really know him, but I definitely felt better after that hug. He said there was solid research on the need to get three hugs a day to be balanced emotionally. He was a hug evangelist and I quickly converted.

Steps in the Bonding Sequence

Dr. Joy studied the work of zoologist, Desmond Morris, on perfectly bonded species (they mate for life) versus all the others. He theorized that successful human bonding follows a similar sequence of development that goes something like this.

Stage One: the Eureka Look. "Eureka!" is an exclamation that means "I found it!" Eureka! We have found something valuable and we celebrate that experience. At the initial stage in the bond we spot something special in another person that separates them from the sea of humanity around them. It's just a little "Ping!" that goes off inside us causing us to see the potential and giftedness in another person. It is an idealized version of the other person, not really an accurate understanding but the spark that makes you want to know them more. Eureka is where you see the possibilities in the other person.

Stage Two: Eye to Eye Contact. Since the eyes are the window of the soul, emotional energy begins to flow between us when we make eye contact. We become linked (networked together to use a computer analogy) and communication begins to flow.

Stage Three: Voice to Voice. The bond progresses as we begin to exchange communications. We pass words, feelings and self-revelation back and forth. We have so much to talk about because, in our eureka moment, we have determined that this other person will be valuable and important in our life.

Stage Four: Hand to Hand. The first casual (non-sexual) touch takes this relationship to a much deeper level. Every relationship needs a certain amount of physical touch to grow deeper. Holding hands, hugging, playing and wrestling, just touching in general, causes the bond to reach our soul. Humans need healthy touch. We bond with those we touch and who touch us.

Stage Five: Arm around Shoulder. Relationships we value are relationships we stand up for in public. Arm around shoulder is the universal symbol of ownership, public notice of a valued relationship. It might be evidenced in other ways too like wearing your team jersey, posting something positive online or introducing your child, friend or marriage partner to others face to face. Family pride is an important part of a deeper bond. A bonded family is proud of their family and its name.

How to Build a Bonded Family

While this sequence has great implications for building and sustaining a warm bond in marriage, it is equally important in building lasting friendships and for parenting a bonded family. Let's look at some examples, going over it again.

Stage One: the Eureka Look. To establish a bond in stage one, we need to maintain our eureka vision of each child. No matter the struggles we might have with them, we need to make sure that in the quiet depth of our heart we do not allow a bitter negative seed to grow. This child is a wonder and a gift and our mind needs to ponder that fact every day. We need to see every member of our family as someone we really need and want to know—and someone we want to reveal ourselves to as well.

Stage Two: Eye to Eye Contact. We need to look our kids in the eye when we speak with them. When they were younger, our children would sometimes become frustrated while trying to speak to us because we were online, reading or working at something while we talked with them. Sherry might hear them say, "Mom, you aren't listening to me!" She would reply, "Sure I am. Here's what you just said…." Then they would reply, "You aren't listening. You aren't looking at me." She knew that she needed to turn to face them and look them in the eyes. Then they knew they were being heard. Knowing how to bond is in our DNA if we pay attention to that little voice in our head (or standing by our knee).

Stage Three: Voice to Voice. To do a better job in bonding at this level, we need to slow down our pace and create some space for talking at length with our kids. These are not scheduled times with an agenda, but hanging-out times, giving them the gift of time. Talking to them easily and listening carefully to what is on their hearts. (Sherry and I found that we could easily run through each day as a family, yet, never really stop to enjoy fellowship and conversation with each other.)

Stage Four: Hand to Hand. This stage is brought about through casual touch. Families need a big king-sized family bed and a large sofa in the TV room for snuggling. Every member of the family needs more touch than they probably get and even if your birth family didn't express love openly, you can learn to do it and enjoy it. Bonded families touch. Touch is what bonds them. It's a circle.

I once led a men's Bible study group and, as my habit was, I hugged everyone who arrived. One man, Jim, stiffened like a board when I hugged him. He said he was from Ireland and that his family didn't do such things. I smiled and told him, "You'll get used to it." He was a little less stiff the next time or two. I started thinking that maybe I was pushing him too much and should just lay off and shake his hand or something the next time we met.

Then I heard his booming voice call, "Chuckie!" as he entered the hall one morning. I turned and saw his arms wide open. As we men shared breakfast that morning he said, "I finally realized that I looked forward to this meeting all week and that it was partly because of these hugs you guys do. It is my only source of touch for the week and I've decided that I need it."

Stage Five: Public Notice--Arm around Shoulder. Level five bonding deals with our security and belongingness needs. Taking the family bond to this level requires that we show our approval and pride in each family member in front of others. Introducing your children to others is a great opportunity to build their confidence but, more importantly, it's a way of saying to your child that they are approved by you and that you are proud to stand beside them in public. Because we stand up for each other in public we know that we truly belong and that our acceptance is a settled fact.

Teaching Children How to Love

Raising children who know how to give and receive love is a joyful undertaking. It starts with how you greet them every time you've been apart or asleep. Kids are just so kissable. (Swapping wild hugs and kisses from children is one of the main benefits in having them anyway.) Our goal was that our kids would be more friendly and openly affectionate than most in whatever culture we served. Some kids take to this naturally and others have to be helped a bit.

One of our children wasn't very affectionate as a child. He seemed almost dismissive of others and seldom made physical gestures of affection. Rather than fret about it, we just added it to the list of things for him to do each day (more on the daily checklist in the chapter on discipline). He had a daily assignment list with an item that read, "Look every family member in the eye every day, then say "I love you," and give them a hug."

At the end of each day we asked him in front of others, "Did you tell everyone that you loved them and did you give them a hug?" "Yes!" he might reply. "No he didn't!" his sister might counter, "He didn't hug me." "I forgot," he might respond. "Well, you'd better give her a hug right now so we can give you a check mark there."

It starts as external, but it works its way inside. It took a few weeks, but our son learned to really enjoy hugs. He was a genius at so many things, but just hadn't mastered love's signals. Rather than just saying, "Oh, I guess he's just less demonstrative," we decided to help him learn the wonderful language of love. If he was stumped at math we would have tutored him on that, so why not on something as important as learning how to show and receive affection.

Getting positive touch and feedback every single day about his hugs helped him feel relaxed and confident about interacting in this way. Gradually, he internalized the lesson and became as affectionate and loving a person as you would ever hope to know. To this day, although he is grown man with two children of his own, Sherry and I both get a hug and kiss on the cheek from him every time we greet.

CHAPTER NINE
BLOCKING TIME FOR YOUR MARRIAGE

Prioritizing Your Own Bond as a Couple

As our children multiplied, along with the scope of our duties at work, we felt the drain on our emotions and our connection as a couple. We realized that if we wanted to create a powerful bond of love within our family, it would depend upon our diligence in maintaining the bond between the two of us. After all, it was our love as a couple that had brought our family into existence in the first place. Not only that, our bond had also allowed our family to expand to include many others who had come to consider themselves Quinleys as well. Though they didn't share our last name they were often at the table with us and spent many nights under our roof.

All of these drew their sense of security from the strength of the bond between Sherry and me. If we broke down it would affect everyone else for life. We began to prioritize time alone at the peak of our parenting load, when we had four kids in elementary school. At this point I also had two full-time jobs. The pressures we were under demanded that even more time be set aside for our replenishment. The old formula is, "When your output exceeds your intake, your upkeep will be your downfall." Meaning? If you intend to take care of others you have to take care of yourself and make certain that you are taking into your soul more life than you are giving out to others.

Once, one of our four girls asked me the mischievous question, "Who do you love more, Mommy or me?" Without hesitation I told her that Mommy was my girlfriend before she ever existed and that it was our love that had created her. "Furthermore," I said, "when you get older, you will leave me and move into your own life, but Mom will be right here by my side, feeding me spoons of oatmeal when all my teeth are gone. We'll be in love forever." Although she might have hoped for a different reply, this answer made her smile and nod her head in agreement. Even at five years of age, she knew that this was the way things should be in a healthy family.

Every child's greatest fear is the loss of their parents either through death or, more commonly, through divorce. Your love as a couple is what led to their existence in the first place and your love is the ground of their stability. Even more, your love together is a prophecy about their marriage one day. Your bond is the model they will follow as they work to establish a healthy one-flesh relationship of their own one day. A solidly-bonded couple is the foundation upon which everyone's security is built in a family. We wanted to hear our children say as young adults, "I want my parents' marriage!" Living with us and watching how we maintained our own bond would help guide them so they could find the kind of love we enjoyed.

Exploring the sights and smells of the world on motorcycles.

Anything you want to cultivate in your life needs an allotment of time dedicated to it. This is true for your health, career advancement or your marriage. In those seasons when we have diligently followed what we're about to share, our marriage has been rock solid and vibrant, despite the challenges we have faced from our own kids and from the load of ministry we bear as we serve the outside world. On the flip side, whenever we have allowed other things to crowd out these priorities we have felt the bond between us loosen and our worst selves have come out (we all have a Dr. Jekyll and Mr. Hyde thing going on, you know). Getting it right and keeping the bond between us growing stronger deserves generous allotments of designated time.

Here's the formula we have followed:

1. Daily: One hour of unbroken time together in bed to process the day we just finished and to reconnect with each other. This can't start till the kids are all locked in. This is not TV watching time, it's time to talk while we sip a drink and have a savory snack.

2. Weekly: One date per week, something special to go and do, just the two of us, no other couples and none of our kids invited. Another of our girls once complained about the unfairness of not getting to go with us on our dates so I explained it to her, "Mom is not just my wife, she's my girlfriend. She works hard for you and she deserves this special time with me. You all get your special times too." She still wanted to join us because it was clear that we were off to have some fun, but had to agree with the logic. Kids may yell, "Yuk!" when they see you kiss, but secretly they are happy to see the love between you. Romantic love needs time to stay healthy. For us, that time is one date per week, whether it needs to be morning, noon or night.

3. Quarterly: We spent one night together away from the kids each three months. That's four times a year. (Before you cry out, "We can't afford 24-hour babysitting!" let us suggest that you find another couple who also wants an awesome marriage and work out a way to help relieve each other for such times. If they have kids the same age as yours it's not that hard to watch them because they just play together.) Getting away from the house and from your duties as parents, even for one night, will be something you look forward to months in advance. This is especially true if the wife plays the role of stay-at-home mom. She need's the tension release, even if she protests and says she's OK.

4. Annually: This was the big one. We spent one week away each year alone. This works well as your annual anniversary trip. It is depressing to ask a couple how they spent their anniversary and have them say, "Oh, it was just an ordinary day." The anniversary of your covenant is the high point of the family year. It is the place where it all started and it must be celebrated and honored especially. It deserves a savings account and a huge amount of planning. Sherry always reminds women she's mentoring, "By the way, the anniversary is not a second birthday for the wife. It isn't her big day to be wowed again. It's your joint celebration to remember and renew your covenant together."

A grand trip together allows you the luxury of time to relax in each other's arms and to reflect on how the past year has gone. This is the time to make a plan to change whatever is needed to make things better in the year ahead. Discuss each child and make your plans for developing their strengths. Discuss where you are financially as a family and talk about the budget needs for the next year and how you will work together on it. Apologize for anything that as been left unspoken in the past year. These things don't go away by ignoring them. You each know where you have failed each other. This trip is the time to reset your marriage.

It's also time to pray together. Ask the Lord what need He would have you give money to as a family and how you could better serve Him. There is much in each year to celebrate and to talk about. There is lots of love to make so these unhurried days should be the highlight and cornerstone for your calendar each year.

Don't say that this is impossible. God will make a way if you will do the work needed. Just buy a blank calendar and sit down together as a couple. (Bring your work and personal schedules with you.) Now, look for the spaces on the calendar where you can drill down and anchor the four time commitments we just mentioned. It might not be easy to execute the first time but work together to solve problems and make it happen (we're back to intentionality).

Here's how one side of the conversation might sound, "Ok, let's block off at least five days for our anniversary and take a little trip this year. We need to figure out where we'd like to go, how much money it will require and who will watch the kids while we are away. Let's set that up now, way in advance, so its secure. These dates should work. Great! Now, we need to mark off three other overnights for us about every three months. This will be so refreshing! Got it locked in? OK, now, what's the best time of the week for a date of about four hours? Check! Now for the daily time, what is the best clearing hour each day so we can have one unbroken hour to stay connected without TV, laptops or phones? What time do we need to commit to being in bed with each other in order to still have an hour of quiet together till we need to be asleep?"

Lock it in then use your will to execute the plan. This one change alone will add so much quality to your life as a married couple. Once you experience the difference it makes you will never want to go back to your old treadmill way of living. Your unity will improve and together you can blast through challenges that rise up before you. Build a bond of steel.

CHAPTER TEN
ENTERTAINMENT VERSUS HOSPITALITY

Sherry and I believe that love is inclusive by its very nature and isn't intended to create a private love club reserved for our nuclear family alone. We wanted to be known as a family where there was always an empty chair at the table and a front door standing open to the world.

One day Sherry came into the house all excited. She held something in her hand. On our journey to having an open home, God had provided us a book. (Has He ever done that for you? Given you a book that perfectly connects to your current need?) The book was entitled, Open Heart, Open Home by Karen Burton-Mains. In it she describes her journey from entertaining to showing true hospitality.

She opens with the story of her house in all it's glory, the perfect shrine to honor her skills as a homemaker. Everything was clean. Colors coordinated well and, of course, everything smelled great. Part of running a model home is entertaining guests, but in an entertaining household, guests should come only when invited. Much preparation must be accomplished before their arrival. The meal should be planned and if the guests will stay overnight, their room should be lavishly appointed with soaps and a bowl of fruit. This, she explained, is the nature of entertaining. It's all about spotlighting you as the gracious host. The goal of entertaining is to demonstrate your hosting skills and to impress your guests.

Karen Mains said that one day her son invited the little boy next door to come and play. The next thing she knew there were grimy little mud tracks from that careless kid's shoes all over the living room carpet. She was mortified and went to work down on her knees scrubbing out the stubborn dirt out before it stained the carpet permanently. She was irritated, but was trying to control her temper when the Lord spoke to her. "Whose house is this anyway?"

God began to show her that, unlike entertaining, hospitality is concerned about the needs of the guest God has brought into your home. It's not about you. It's about them. They may need to come by when it's not convenient for you. You may not always have time to perfect the appearance of your house. Precious things might become worn out or even broken through the practice of showing hospitality. The point is to focus on meeting the practical needs of your guest, not on impressing them that you are super host. Once you can shift from entertaining others to showing them hospitality, God can begin to use your home as the center for a powerful ministry. It's an important thought. We recommend Open Heart, Open Home. It's a great book for you to buy and read for yourself.

Cozy Chaos

The most hospitality we had ever felt in our earliest days as a couple was in the home of John and Kathy Simmons. John taught art at Lee University where we both attended. Kathy was mother to four small kids, two girls, two boys (that alone amazed us) and was homeschooling them. The kids were artistic like their father but with four active kids bouncing off the walls and their art supplies and half finished projects strewn about, their house couldn't have the orderly silence of an art gallery. The energy in the house was permanently set at a positive buzz, like a nuclear reactor humming happily away in the background. Now you would think that a mom with four homeschooling kids would have her hands full and you would be absolutely correct, yet we always knew that the door to Kathy's kitchen was going to be unlocked and that surprise visitors were typically a delight to her.

She always seemed to have a big pot of soup on the stove "just in case" and could hold a baby on her hip, drink coffee and really listen to you despite the din of ninja boys wrestling in the hallway. She never seemed embarrassed about the shoes and coats thrown about. She would just tell you to "shove that stuff off the sofa and find a place to sit." If she needed help washing dishes while we talked, she wasn't shy to ask for it or even to tell you that she was on her way out and you might have to come back another time. The point was that you felt seen, welcomed, and accepted. Her home was magnetic. Dozens of students were irresistibly drawn there.

The amazing thing to both of us was the way Kathy could tune in to anyone who passed through her door. Stepping inside the door to her home you had entered her sacred space and God did much good work in there. She saw you, saw down deep inside you, but she was safe and you felt such nurture coming from her. She prayed for people and helped carry the load

Julia with her scholar and playmate, Erika.

Jessica during her Summer of service with ARM. She missed going to Yellowstone because she was committed to these kids.

The girls helping plant rice.

you were bearing. We wanted to be like Kathy and John.

A family is a love factory. Sherry and I determined that we would also open the door of our house to the world and let love do its work in the lives of those outside our family. Becoming an open family started by including the playmates of our children. We bought extra food and made them feel they were always welcome in our home. Then we extended it from there into the families of those children. Finally, we began to welcome into our home, people we had met only that day.

More than any other single practice, opening up our home as a place of refuge changed us. It stretched and deepened our hearts to care more for others and to see our home as a place of healing waters. Some guests stayed for dinner. Others stayed for six months. It was not a burden to us generally. We accepted that this was precisely the reason God had given us all our extra stuff.

Our children, as a consequence of this lifestyle, have all chosen a life of ministry in some form or other. They "see" people, and they have had decades of observation and practice with informal counseling. They have seen the healing power that flows from healthy people into those who need that strength. It works by osmosis. Our kids came to understand this. They see themselves as healthy, wealthy and strong. They are strong because they minister to others. Through experience they have discovered that their needs will always be met and they will have more than enough clothes, food and bed space to share. That's God's math. He takes care of those who take care of others.

Black Holes

The bottom line is that selfish families can't become great families no matter how hard they try. They are like a great black hole because they make themselves and their impressive, private house the center of their universe. Black holes, it turns out, are actually bright stars that have such a powerful gravitational self-focus that they suck in all the light they could have shone on others. We are determined to make good on that kindergarten song, "This little light of mine, I'm going to let it shine."

SECTION THREE

The Control Years

The "largeness" of your child's life will ultimately come from how hard they work, how well they use their gifts, and how boldly they act when opportunities present themselves. Building their adult life is something kids will have to do for themselves, but the shaping of their character is a different matter entirely. It is the work of the adults who raise them. This is a huge responsibility and it is the central task of parenting. The question that should burn in every parent's heart needs to be "How can I help build strong character in my child?" That is the question we will now attempt to answer.

CHAPTER ELEVEN
THE PARENTING PARADIGM

This brings us to the core idea of this little book. It's a simple thought, but is the single-most-important concept we ever received about the workflow of parenting. Our friend, Allen, heard it from a man who ran a home for out-of-control teens. Allen drew a diagram on a napkin at dinner one night and the task of parenting became simple to us. We were grateful to have received this insight while our kids were still so young. Throughout our days as parents, we committed ourselves to work it. Now, we pass it on to you.

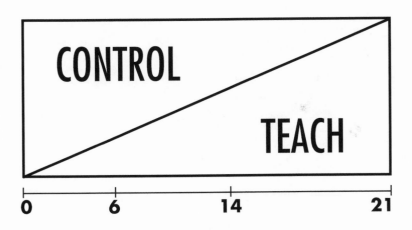

A One Way Street

Let's unpack this simple drawing. The one predictable thing about parenting is that your child's development only moves in one direction. Time moves things to the right of the chart and the parenting task changes gradually along the way in response.

Parenting has two main tasks and these are strictly sequential. The first task of a parent is simply the impartation of control upon the child. This control is first external, then gradually becomes set internally as the child develops autonomous control over time.

Nothing else can happen until control over the child's will is established. The window for establishing this control is small and will close a little with each of their birthdays.

In the early days of parenting there is little teaching. This develops later. Before teaching can happen a child must submit to be taught. They have to become teachable. Teachability is the key to excellence and continued growth throughout life. We can arm our children with this vital lifelong character trait by teaching them to learn from those who are years ahead of them in life.

A Brief Window of Opportunity

As parents we can gain control while kids are in their earliest years because, well, we are giants compared to them. We're just huge in every way. Everything they want and need has to pass through us and that gives us tremendous power for a brief season.

At this stage they also have no prior programming to overcome. They have nothing to unlearn. They have few relationships and no other loyalties in their lives. Just us. This unique and unrepeatable opportunity gives us a chance to become the rudder for their lives until they become mature enough to take the rudder from us and guide themselves.

While they are still young enough to be pliable, we need to bend their will so it will ultimately set in the right place and will reliably point them toward a future that is healthy and secure.

The Bible says that the problem with the earth is the poison of sin that lies within us. No one teaches a child to lie. They just do at some point. No one teaches them to rebel against authority either, but if you tell a two year old not to cross the line you draw in the sand it won't be long until they creep to that line and move their stubby little toe just on the other side.

This sin nature is rooted in the self. We center our world on ourself and we crave to be little gods with nobody telling us what to do. As difficult as it is to do, a loving parent has to confront the rebellion and sin in their own precious child and bring that child's will under control so the lifetime work of true parenting can begin. James Dobson's classics, <u>The Strong Willed Child</u> and <u>Dare to Discipline</u> were very helpful to us in this stage of our parenting journey.

If we don't bend the will of a young child and point it beyond the petty concerns of the self, it will set in the original place and they will become a predominantly selfish person. Selfish people are sad, frustrated people. The world never seems to understand how important they are. They never get what they "deserve" though they often rant about it. Training the self-centered will to become more selfless requires constant, unyielding pressure.

When a baby learns to say what they want, the baby becomes a child. When a child learns to subordinate what they want to the greater needs of others, the child becomes an adult. The control years are the first step along this process.

But I Want Longer Control!

In the first stage of your child's life, getting them under your control is all you need to think about. Some parents want to extend the stage of total control beyond the first six years. They'd like complete control for all twenty years their child will be with them. It's possible to extend total control for a few more years, but it's not natural. We could keep them ignorant, keep them broke, and keep them away from others who might empower them, but no healthy parent would want that for their child. We want them to be strong, right?

In our heart, Sherry and I long for our children to go far beyond us. We will give them all that we have as their starting point so that their life's "zero" will begin at our lifetime best. They get to start from there. That's their legacy. This is how a family grows from strength to strength throughout generations, and becomes a dynasty. The strength in a child is our friend. We want to see them growing stronger and more capable every year. Establish firm controls in the earliest days of your child's life and they will willingly follow you out of respect later when they can stand alone and you have no real power over them.

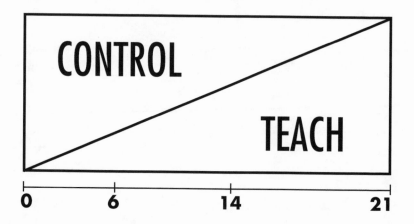

A New Role Emerges

The waning of your ability to exert total control coincides with the birth of a wonderful, new role in your child's life, that of teacher and mentor. This mentoring role starts gradually, overshadowed, at first, by your existing role of controller. Teaching continues to deepen and overshadow your controlling function over time. The good news is that the teacher's role can be yours for life. There will always be a place for you in their lives if you can make the transition away from power at the appropriate point in your life together.

Vertical power in a relationship actually hinders the free flow of communion between two people. It's hard to be a true friend with someone who has power over you. Some parents, longing for this deeper level of power-free connection with their children, try to move too quickly to teacher/mentor/friend only to be replaced by new authorities (peers, teachers, songwriters, authors) who crowd into their child's life in their teen years. This relegates the parent to something of a chaplain, a far cry from the place of influence they could have had.

The King Who Lost His Throne

There is an old story of a king who came to his top general and said, "I hate punishing people. You do it. I'll be the nice guy who gives out the rewards." Six months later the king called for a second meeting saying, "I don't understand it. Now everyone snaps to attention when you walk by, but I have to beg them to obey. Despite all my generosity and love, nobody seems to honor me any more. We're going to change roles. I'll harden up and be the one who demands law and order. You lighten up and be the rewarder." The end of the story is that in another six months the general became king.

A firm leader can always lighten up once people are flowing well under his authority. Everyone will then say, "I thought she was stern, but she's really open and loving." On the other hand, if you have been permissive for years, don't think you will be able to grab the reins of control and pull back hard on a child without consequences.

Let the sequence take its course naturally. First establish yourself as God's representative authority and guardian, the ultimate adult in their world and the one due the highest respect. From that strong position it is an easy thing to shift to a role of lower control. The point is to do this voluntarily and responsively as your child earns liberty and not to have it stripped from you against your will and better judgment.

The Glory of Becoming a Teacher

Teachers as a professional group bear the most influence in the lives they engage. They don't have the most raw power, but they often change the course of a student's life. Many doctors begin their story of how they entered the field of medicine with, "I had this chemistry teacher in the ninth grade..."

Influence does not require power and control. That's the wonderful part about the second stage of parenting. If you have done a great job in the first phase of parenting you'll have their respect. Then you can gradually release controls to the child, take the passenger seat and teach them how to make friends, how to drive, how to take tests, how to get a raise at work, etc. There are so many things we all want to teach our children about life and if we can successfully cross the midway boundary, the relational energy between us can be redirected into a teaching/mentoring mode instead of burning it up in an attempt to maintain controls indefinitely.

That's the path we've learned to follow. We controlled firmly while we could, then transitioned smoothly and gradually to a role of decreasing control in favor of cheerleading and coaching from the shadows backstage. We found that if we kept ourselves growing after our kids left home, we continued to hold a permanent position as the source of wisdom in the lives of our adult children as well.

CHAPTER TWELVE
SIX MAGIC YEARS

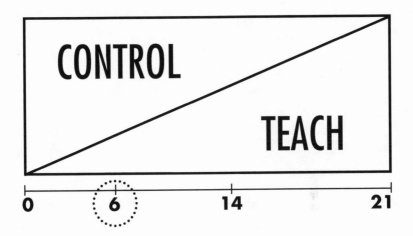

You basically have six magic years to establish control over a child. As your child grows physically larger, mentally smarter, more verbal and socially connected with resources in the outside world (food, money, places to stay, etc.), they will gradually gain for themselves the elements that give you power over them in the beginning.

Eventually, you will lose all true control of your children and this is not a bad thing. It will slip away from you gradually no matter how hard you try to hold onto it (and by all means do hold on as long as you can). Once it has been lost, especially on a teen, you can hardly regain control without shedding blood. I'm joking, but it's almost that hard. Sure, you can lock them in their room, but they can escape out the window. (Don't laugh, some parents have actually tried this). Control slips away along with the passing of sand through the hourglass. Even in a healthy family, parents maintain control of their teens only because the teens have accepted in childhood that parents have the right to sit in authority over them. They submit to control from their heart, not because we can really impose it on them externally.

In their teens, even healthy kids come to realize that they are as physically strong as most adults, and have survival resources of their own. Still, they accept that it is best for them to allow their parents to set boundaries for them. They (more or less) obey us even when they think we are wrong, because they have yielded control of their lives to us and don't usually intend to take it back before leaving home.

There is only one stage in your child's development when you truly have control over them and it's in their first six years because, again, you are huge in every way compared to them. Your weight is five to ten times theirs. You are able to effortlessly snatch them off the ground by the back of their shirt. You can hold them down with one hand. In those days parents control everything about their child's survival and emotional security. Every meal, all clothing and everything else that is necessary and enjoyable comes from the parents. By God's design a parent can dominate every area of their world for a very, very brief, six-year period of time, about 20% of their life with you in the home.

This isn't the time to be their equal buddy. While you still can, work diligently to establish your authority and control over them. By the time your child turns four you should be able to say to them, "Sit on that chair till I come and get you, ok?" and find them there thirty minutes later. If you say, "Make up your bed," or "Greet Mrs. Johnson," "Turn off the TV," or "Hand me your video game," they should hop up and do just that without a word.

Heed the Warning

Here's the warning, young parents, and please take it seriously because we know what we are talking about. If you fail to establish firm, unquestioned parental control by a child's sixth birthday, the odds are that you will never have it. This means that you can look forward to their transformation into a self-centered, unreasonable teenager who increasingly dominates you as they grow older and stronger. It will be difficult for you to truly enjoy this child or have any meaningful part in their lives when they become young adults because they will make their decisions with only their tiny concerns at the center. They will become lords of their own world and of yours too if you let them.

By the time insubordinate children reach their mid teens most of their parents are in such a weak position that they begin counting the days until their child leaves. Many will put their fourteen-year-old daughters on birth control. To avoid conflict, such parents usually give resistant kids total autonomy. These parents surrender their leadership with the tired sigh, "It's your life. Mess it up if you want to but you have to live with it." Lack of accountability to parental authority will then give these teens the opportunity to experiment with the darker things in life. Inevitably they will suffer from their choices and the cycle will continue in the next generation as well.

But wait! There's more! In a control-free house the fun is not over yet. Tens of thousands of parents have become cast members in their own personal soap opera as their dysfunctional adult children, now in their twenties, thirties and beyond return to live with them again, bringing all their chaos with them. Many of these adult children will have troubles with unplanned pregnancies and substance-abuse. They will complain that they can't provide for themselves or hold down a steady job. They may even blame their parents for the injustice of their situation. In part, they may be right. The root issue in most of these sad cases is that their parents simply failed to establish adult control over them in the first six years of their lives. They were never taught to willingly function under authority so they now have issues with God, bosses, and the police.

It doesn't have to be like this. We know from experience that you can get up every day loving to be a parent. You can take your kids to the store without them throwing a tantrum in the candy aisle. They can be trained to sit quietly on a chair while you have an important conversation with an adult friend. You can even truly enjoy all of your child's teenage years and fully trust them to be where they promise to be going in the family car, but this is possible only if you have established submission in the heart of your child while they are still a preschooler. Parents can pay a little bit in these first six years or pay big later and keep on paying throughout life.

CHAPTER THIRTEEN
BEAGLES AND BABIES

Ten years ago we bought a beagle. We've had many dogs through the years and we thought beagles were cute so we got one without doing much research. Ours chewed up all the furniture and would not listen to instruction. Worse, the dog seemed to have no bond with us. He just wanted our food. This was strange as every pet we'd ever had showed a strong emotional connection.

We finally bought a book on the care and training of beagles. It said something like this,

> *"Every encounter with your beagle is a training moment. You are training him what to expect from you and he is training you in what he wants. If you will take charge of your dog it will have a happy life because it will behave and will fit in nicely with your family. Your beagle will feel loved because you will seldom need to correct it. You will take your beagle with you on trips and together you will enjoy the sights and smells of the great outdoors. A properly trained dog will love and protect his master for life.*

> *If, however, you allow this beagle to train you, you are in for a long, miserable experience as a dog owner. It is one of the most independent of all dog breeds and will be a constant source of frustration for you. The unfortunate beagle will live with the feeling of being unloved and rejected due to the constant scoldings that mark*

each day. Because of his constant misbehavior people will not want him to be around, and he will live a lonely life because of his isolation from the world of his family."

When I read it, I thought, "He's talking about kids."

These days it's common to watch earnest mothers engage their three-year-olds in long, sincere teachings about why we don't bite other children. They use powerful logic like, "It makes them sad." Three-year-olds don't need a lot of discussion. Time for long conversations will come, but in these early years it needs to be pure control, reward and punishment. There is so much you will want to teach your child, but as any public school teacher can tell you, there is no teaching until you first gain control of your students.

Does Restraining my Child Damage Them?

Some may be concerned about the potential damage of restraining a child. Nonsense. We restrain kids all the time. Child restraints are built into every car. We have to restrain them. Children are born without internal controls. For example, they have no bladder or bowel control when they are born. Do we let them run wild and free, unrestrained to follow whatever feels right to them? Not in the house at least. Why not? Because their lack of internal control leads to messes we don't want to keep cleaning up. We are not going to live in a house with poop piles all over the place, so, whether they like it or not, we lay them on their backs and strap on a diaper, an external control.

Internal controls will gradually develop but they take time. You'll know it's time to potty train when your baby wakes up in the morning with a dry diaper. They are gaining internal bladder control, so we can do away with the need for external controls like diapers.

This is the primary spiritual goal of the first stage of parenting—establishing firm external controls and holding them in place until internal controls grow up around them.

More than Diapers

Establishing external control is not just about diapers. It is essential in all matters dealing with conscience and character. At birth, a child does not know right from wrong. Their character is soft and easy to shape. Consequently, when they are very small we want to dominate their lives completely in love and install a system of morals and ethics to guide their behavior. For this to work, our children need the same set of trusted caregivers with them for their first four years. The system around them needs to keep to the same standard every day. They need us to stay close to them physically to touch, love, play, sing, tell them stories.

To avoid someone planting a moral virus in their minds we need to control 100% of the content of their media mind food. They need constant communication about the things we want them to love and those we want them to avoid. These are the days when we need to set and enforce predictable standards in our home.

The perceptual end goal of this season can be conceived of as building mass for yourself in the eyes of your children. You will want to become a huge mountain in their lives, an unmovable landmark they can always have as a reliable guide.

Young kids have to become convinced quickly that they cannot move us with their will, defiance, humor or charm. We are the mountain and they have to yield to us. They must do what we say without questioning us. They can do it out of respect, love or a reasonable fear of the consequences, but they must do it, nonetheless. Sherry and I consistently communicated the basic rules regarding our relationship with them. They would obey us, show us appropriate respect, and tell us the truth when we questioned them. We also communicated that if they would do their part, then we could take good care of them and their lives would be happy and we would have a lot of fun together.

Obedience and respect are important character traits for many reasons. The greatest reason is that as parents, we are God's represented authority in their lives. If they learn to obey, respect and love us they will also love

Him. If they rebel against us, they are rebelling against Him too and will do so even more as they gain more autonomy. This forms the primary curriculum for ages one through six. We want to establish the "fear of the Lord" that the scripture says is the beginning of all wisdom.

But Will They Love Me?

There will be battles during this period. The "terrible twos" are famous worldwide as a season when the will of the child asserts itself against yours and they attempt to gain mastery over you. Some parents totally lose it here and become weak. "But they won't love me if I discipline them!" they protest.

Let's remember that all of us had to teach our kids to even mouth the words "I love you." Whenever they said these words to us we rewarded them because we want them to learn to give and receive love, but also because we like to hear them say this to us. Small children are a swirl of new and frighteningly-fluid emotions. Sometimes they are sweet but then they can go into squalling fits, the kind when their eyes roll back in their head like a scene from the exorcist.

They do not yet have the full emotional capacity to even know what love is so we can't hang our lives on whether our three year old pouts when we discipline them. A child only knows that they like to get their way. They like people who give them gifts and special treats and who don't restrain them. Resist their will and they won't like it. Being childish, they will show it in many ways. Stand firm. These days won't last forever if you win unchallenged authority by their sixth birthday.

At this first stage in the game, we just wanted our kids' respect and obedience. As humans we do not love those we do not respect. We reasoned that our children would truly love us when they were mature enough to know what love really was. As it turned out, this didn't really take long at all.

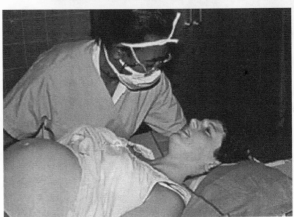

From the top
Love drunk in our college days.

Early days at Blue Hole in the Smokey Mountain chain. We met at Lee University.

Amazingly, the nurse is saying "Don't push!" She was afraid the doctor would be mad if the baby was already born by the time he arrived. He couldn't charge a delivery fee in that case.

Early days, Jamaica.

Red earth, red kids,
at least till bath time

Kristin's
1st Bday

It tickles when they eat out of your hand!

Reina has been in our family
for the past twenty years and
serves in ministry with us in
Thailand even now.

Little Nathan thinking
about that first jump.

Brooke, waking slowly on her birthday.

Jessica getting her legs
shaved for the first time.

Why kids need time in the woods:
Brooke and Julia seeing how loud and long
they can scream in each other's face.

Brooke makes a friend in Nepal.

220 lb. Python in Thailand.

Jacki and Julia with Joann's kids in a Manila barrio.

It takes a village to raise a child. Our six have grown up surrounded by many loving adults

Our girls were always the center of attention among the hill tribes.

Kristin and a friend in Japan trying to master the face.

Big brothers can be a pillar of strength and protection for sisters if they take their role seriously. Andrew has been diligent about it.

Sherry and her parents, Sam and Audrey before Sam passed away.

Our family circa 2012.

My Dad and Mom on a visit to Thailand. They served with us for four years in the Philippines.

Jessica and Nathan ready to surprise
Brooke at school for her birthday.

Cake in the cafeteria
for Brooke's 16th.

Andrew reads dramatic scenes to inspire
Jessica's abstract work on art day.

Two days moving slowly upriver
in Laos, but still smiling.

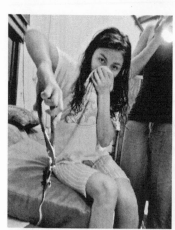

Dead reptiles burrowed
inside the sofa.
Tropical problems.

Working with Robin Kung in Myanmar, setting up an amputation and prosthetic for a man with a hopelessly twisted leg. Now he has his first job and is supporting his family.

Joann Luciano and some of the 9,000 children she reaches weekly.

Julia as "the White Akha."
It took 45 minutes to put the head dress on.

Sharing a meal with a Burmese family

Andrew's wedding rehearsal dinner meltdown. It was the first time anyone had left the inner circle for a life on their own.

Jacki gave us August, our first grandson then Reese, our first granddaughter, all in two years. So glad they live down the street from us!

Kristin & Jason were playmates when they were two years old in Jamaica. She met him again in Portland in her late twenties. They married one year later.

Jessica was the first daughter to marry. Ben's mom has been Sherry's best girlfriend for the past 30 years. Mamma magic working!

Nathan with Rebekah, before they married.

Tea at sunset, a lifetime tradition.

CHAPTER FOURTEEN
THE CENTRAL TASK OF PARENTING

All too soon your baby grows into a child. Along with this physical growth comes rapid intellectual development. It's amazing to watch two-year-olds whip through apps on an iPhone and repeat the names of everyone in a room though they just met them that day. The mind isn't the only thing in development though. Your child's character, at first a loose collection of responses to their inner impulses, begins to slowly take shape. The child begins to develop habitual patterns of thinking and acting.

Like cement, once it is set, your child's character will be difficult to change. That's why the central task of parenting in the control years is the establishment of a set of external and internal controls. Using these controls we can shape their character positively during its formation.

An Inner Core of Strength

Building strong backbone in children begins with a set of external controls applied to them without their permission or awareness. It is our sacred duty to them and one that needs diligence in order to work. As we erect this—think of it as a wire mesh structure—in their core, they may resist it at first. Their craving for total autonomy will want to push it out and their love for comfort will not appreciate this work you are doing on their behalf.

If we are diligent and keep things in place even as they wiggle, their own spiritual bone will form around it (OK, think of Wolverine from Marvel comics now). In the end, these external controls will have the positive result of becoming an Adamantium spine of strength within your child's character.

In a world of weaklings who cannot delay their gratification for even the noblest of objectives, your kids will be superheroes. They will succeed at work and at home because of the inner core of strength they possess. One day they will be able to stand on their own against the crowd without wavering, even when you have long passed from this life. Strong character in your child is your gift to the next three generations. Character is formed through discipline.

Shaming, Punishment and Discipline

Shaming, punishment, and discipline are totally separate things. Shaming is the immature action of a damaged person, intent on creating humiliation and internal pain in the soul of another. "I'm ashamed of you," is a sentence that you can never take back and which can never be erased from the psyche of the target person. Shaming puts you down so I can feel superior. It uses our greatest fear, rejection, as a weapon to cow us down in servitude. Shame breaks us down and leaves places of permanent weakness inside, like that nagging sense that we will never be worthy or good enough. It has no place in any family.

One thing I always hated as a pastor were home visits when a well-intentioned mother would say to her child something like, "Marvin, tell Pastor Chuck what you did today" (wanting him to confess some dark deed she had discovered). Life is a huge, heavy load much of the time. If our kids are going to succeed they need to be strong inside, not broken down.

Punishment is focused on the past. It is about setting the scales of justice back in balance. Someone has done something unjust, injuring someone else, and this has tipped the scales toward injustice. To set things right the guilty party needs to fix what they have done in some way that balances the scales again. Punishment should "fit the crime" or you create another injustice by over-punishing and making the guilty party now into a victim of the justice system. (The rule of "an eye for an eye" was established to avoid "a head for an eye.")

We wouldn't say that there should never be punishment in a family. You might need to hold a people's court among children sometimes. They have a very clear sense of justice, often superior to ours, and it's a good exercise for the group to decide a just sentence on Jonny for intentionally ripping the head off of Mary's doll. Common sense, and even Jonny himself, would probably suggest a public apology and that he has to have her doll fixed perfectly or buy her another doll. Fairness is part of justice and justice is what punishment is all about. My Uncle Luther's family had a structured legal system. Hitting your sister had a set judicial penalty, known to all. Before Ernie hit Rhonda, he had to think about the consequences and Rhonda knew as well as Ernie did that there would be payback if he hit her. As a child I thought it was pretty cool and that it was fair.

What Discipline is

Discipline is the higher way because it is focused on the future. It is a relentless pressure, like corrective braces on bowed legs, designed to take what is crooked and make it become straight with the dream of a future where the child strides confidently on strong legs all on her own. Discipline is costly love now, targeted at the future version of this child as an independent adult. It is best accompanied with a speech like, "You are an honest boy. I trust your words and you are good inside. I can hardly believe that you lied to me! We have to get this lying out of you!" Discipline is the gold standard of external control. We need to focus on discipline above all. Let's dig deeper.

Thefreedictionary.com defines discipline in two ways,

> 1. The training expected to produce a specific character or pattern of behavior, especially training that produces moral or mental improvement. 2. Controlled behavior resulting from disciplinary training; self-control.

This definition recognizes two things: first, that discipline is training by external pressure and second that this pressure produces internalized self-control over time.

Cambridge.org says it this way

> [Discipline is] "training that makes people more willing to obey or more able to control themselves..." (emphasis mine).

The Mastery of Life Through Discipline

The pressure of consistent discipline is a prerequisite to mastering anything in life. In academics we call each field of study, "a discipline."

Julia, 18, training for her professional Muay Thai kick boxing match in Thailand.

There is a correct way to hold a pencil, fire a rifle, treat a girl you take to the prom, strike the keys of a piano, pull out in traffic, start off with a new teacher, do a handshake, ride a bicycle, manage money, and apply for a job. The same is true in sports. Golf is not a self-taught sport. Neither is gymnastics or anything else at a world-class level. Discipline is bound up with excellence and must come first before any true mastery is possible. There are hackers and artists. There are professionals and

Julia doing the traditional Wai Kruu dance under the blazing glare of her opponent.

there are hobbyists. The difference is discipline. If Sherry and I wanted our children to excel beyond us in all things, then we needed to get them accustomed to the presence of discipline in their lives as a permanent condition and a welcomed life partner.

Discipline Leads to Overcoming Inhibitions

The problem with training children is that sometimes the adults in charge still have personal stuff they have never dealt with. So, for example, mothers with body-image issues pass these on to their daughters. Fathers with hot tempers pass these on as well.

To be good at discipline, each of us has to do our best to come to grips with our issues and work on being emotionally healthy ourselves. Healthy things grow and growing things change. Sherry and I determined to be good self-managers and to continue to grow and evolve, hopefully, into continually improving versions of ourselves. We need to let discipline do its good work in us daily before we can be useful in applying discipline to our children's lives as well. Don't be discouraged, though, if you feel that you have too many weaknesses to be a good trainer for your own children. Sometimes the presence of a parent's inner weakness can motivate their parental choices in positive ways.

In my case, I was painfully shy in high school. Just thinking about crowds can still cause my hands to break out in sweat. I determined that I would do my best to intentionally root this common insecurity out of our children. Since we are missionaries who have to raise our own support we were presented with the perfect opportunity. Every two or three years we needed to return home to visit our supporting churches in the USA. They generally cleared an entire Sunday service for our presentation. We created a family show for the occasion. Before Sherry and I spoke the children were called to join us onstage to sing (corny, but cute) and then to be part of a canned interview where they could each tell the audience something interesting about their life in Asia.

Kids had to gain the courage and skills to speak to crowds.
Our mission call belongs to us all.

The kids moaned a bit, but we assigned them some funny lines and the people gave them such positive feedback that it was a bearable experience. Over years of doing this they gradually gained the poise to stand confidently in front of crowds of more than a thousand, look them in the eyes, and speak from their own heart with the relaxed air of a professional. All six of our kids are great communicators today. The discipline of being made to stand on the stage gave them confidence in public speaking situations. This will benefit them for the rest of their lives. Without my own nagging public weakness they may never have set foot on a stage, so don't feel bad about your own weaknesses. Just find a way to use them. We are all broken in just the right places anyway. It's our destiny.

CHAPTER FIFTEEN
HOW DO I CONTROL MY YOUNG CHILD?

Whole books have been written on how to establish an overall environment of discipline in the home. There are dozens of things you can do. We'll roll off a list now from our own parenting playlist and make a few comments along the way.

1. Be present in their world as much as you can, for the first four years especially. They need the consistency of the same adults reinforcing the same set of standards from day to day in this first season of their lives. Study them like science until you truly know your child.

2. Control their physical world. Remove anything you don't like from cable TV to sugary sweets to violent toys, so it's just not there to fuss about.

3. Establish and maintain a structured way of life in general. Controlled patterns of life feel secure and minimize a child's impulses to take over. Set times for getting up, eating, exercise, and going to bed. Set times when media use is OK and when it is not. Set times for creative exercises. Establish firm boundaries and resist the child's efforts to move them.

4. Delay gratification on everything as often as you can. For example, if you want to take them to the zoo, announce it, then set the plan on a date somewhere in the future and keep referring to it and learning about it, but don't move it up on the calendar. Make them wait. Then there are the usual rules most parents set, like, they can't play with their friend till they pick up the toys in their rooms, no dessert till they eat their meal, etc. In general, look for any excuse to delay giving them things they want, even for one hour.

5. Require respectful titles for adults and authority figures. Since when did six-year-olds start calling their mother, Debbie? Children should respect authorities and call adults by titles that indicate their roles (Miss, Mister, Aunt, Uncle, Doctor, Officer, etc.). Don't think that this is too old fashioned. It actually works to the child's lifetime advantage. When young people approach adults with respect and ask them for wisdom and guidance, adults typically love it and are delighted at the opportunity to share the wisdom they have gained through experience. Tangible benefits for the young people generally follow. Remember that older adults still hold the keys to the world. Through their extensive network of lifetime contacts they can open amazing doors to jobs and other opportunities in life. Manners are classy in any age and work to the child's advantage throughout life.

6. Exercise them twice daily. All of us have a certain reservoir of negative energy that will come out in our tone of voice and in our attitude. We all need to sweat to get it out. Kids, in particular, have lots of pent-up energy. Much childhood misbehavior will immediately disappear if you'll just chase your kids around the house ten times. In place of watching TV, evenings are a great chance for dads to engage their kids physically and get some exercise while doing it. Wrestle, play active sports or otherwise work your kids into a sweaty, gritty mess, then feed them, pop them in the shower and into their pajamas. Pray with them and watch them drift to a deep contented sleep.

7. Get them off caffeine, sugars and other stimulants. If a child is raised eating carrot sticks they will think them plenty sweet and wonderful. If they never had Coke in their house they will have stronger bones and less dental bills to boot. It's easier for kids (and adults) to control their moods when they aren't on "drugs" so minimize caffeine, sugar and other assorted junk in the family diet. Just don't buy it.

8. Turn off the Electricity. Remove as much electronic stimulation as possible from kids' lives. Somehow it transfers energy and keeps them agitated, sullen and grumpy. They get addicted to iPads and obsess over getting their hands on one. Kids have the rest of their lives to become addicted to video games. Let's give them six healthy years to establish a human pattern of thinking before wiring them to the Matrix for life. Give them books. Read to them as part of your daily routine.

9. Establish a swift, firm response to all willful challenges. This can be the "time out chair," restriction, going to bed, or whatever else the situation demands, but there needs to be an immediate response from you without hesitation. Yes, we were old school and did "pop that bottom" in preschool kids with the caveat that spanking was restricted to acts of defiance and rebellion. We hit the back of the legs or the bottom with an open hand, usually once, never more than three times. We NEVER hit the face and we didn't spank for mistakes, grades or anything else but rebellion. Whatever system you choose, it really does have to be systematic and unwavering. To work as a deterrent, the response of a parent to disrespect must be thoroughly predictable.

We were firm on this with the first two and it had a double benefit. Their being under such good control created an "obedience culture" among all the following children so we hardly spanked the last four. Oh, and one more thing—we didn't give our child "the cold shoulder" after we disciplined them. Some parents let a sense of displeasure linger in the air for hours or even days. We wanted to make sure they knew that we had spanked them because they were too good a child to allow them to behave like that. We often had to help them apologize for their disrespect, but as soon as they did, things were over.

After their sixth year there is little gained by spanking but you'd better devise some kind of response to the smart mouth that shouts "No!" in your face besides pretending to cry. If you deal forcefully with defiance by age four you will probably never have to deal with it again because your authority will be a settled fact.

10. Protect them from outside influences. Later on you'll need to prepare your children to interact with divergent practices and value systems, but for now they simply need protection. Much childhood misbehavior is imported. Your child plays with a neighbor's and sees attitudes and actions that are bold or willful then brings it home to try it out. You can usually tell who is good for your child and who is not if you are watching closely. If you notice a negative change in the tone and manner of your child after spending time with a certain playmate, limit their exposure to that child.

On a related subject, try not to be paranoid about your children being abused, but if there is a danger present it will generally be from people they know and love, not from strangers. Children need to play with other children and adults. This is healthy and necessary. Removing any conditions that could create privacy during these contacts is a good policy. In our house kids did not lock doors and played together with outsiders only with their doors wide open. Privacy predicts trouble. Kids don't need it.

11. Our Secret Weapon: The Daily Checklist. Something that worked wonders with our preschool and elementary-aged children was a daily accountability checklist. We put a sample one in the endnotes of this book. You can easily make your own. It works like this. You sit with your child and make a list of all the actions you want to see from them. Chores, yes, but more than that. Character traits too. At the end of every day we had a family meeting in a bedroom where we took out their worksheet. It was like judgment day, but in a nice way. Every child stood there as we went down the list with their siblings as witnesses. "Did you brush your teeth this morning and tonight?" "Yes!" "Oh Boy! That means a big check mark for you in that box!" The affirmation of being acknowledged every day for all the good things they had done was powerful in shaping their daily pattern of behavior.

12. Stickers!!! This totally surprised us. Now for this incentive to work, stickers need to become a rare and valuable commodity around your house. Sherry was homeschooling them and was looking for ways to reward good work. Stamping "Nice Job" was great but we found that little kids went crazy about peeling off a sticker and putting it on their work. Sherry scouted stores around the world looking for the best stickers ever, and we amassed a respectable assortment of holograms, glow-in-the-dark, and super hero stickers. It was like getting an olympic gold medal. Sometimes we put them on their shirt, their body or on their checklist itself, then posted the trophy on the fridge for all our guests to see. (We prompted guests to notice the worksheets and to praise our kids for them. Praise from Uncles and Aunts is a powerful form of affirmation.)

CHAPTER SIXTEEN
FOUR KINDS OF FAMILIES

When I was working on my doctorate at Asbury we studied family systems. The theory is that families are more than a collection of individuals. They are, in fact, systems that are either functional or dysfunctional as a whole. These systems create certain outcomes as a byproduct. We studied a chart like these below that proposed to describe all families in terms of two axes: love and control. The chart looked like this.

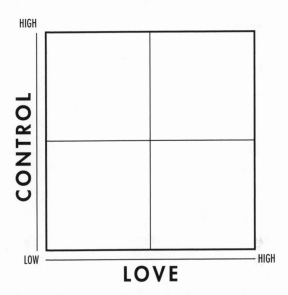

Note that the lower left is where the two axes start. This is the zero point for both love and control in a family. Let's look at the four types of family systems that can be described by placing them in the square relative to the amount of love and control they maintain.

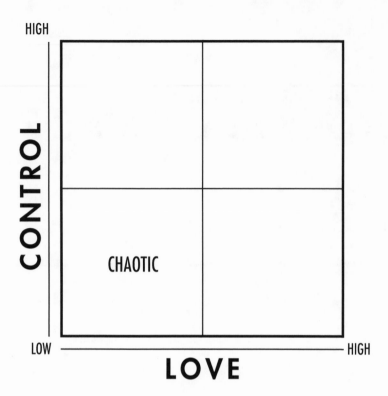

The Chaotic Family

This lower left corner (see above) describes a chaotic family that has little connection among its members. It's like living in a bus terminal. People come and go and might pass in the hall, but they don't seem connected. Missing are the normal expressions of bonding or affection. These family members aren't invested in each other or in the family as a unit. This family also has no functioning system of control, no bedtimes, family meals, discipline, no value system at its core. Nobody seems to care too deeply about the condition of things in this family. There is a clear sense that no one is in charge. It's a mess really. Many substance abuse homes fit this family system, but all chaotic families aren't in circumstances that dramatic. Some are just not well bonded and as a consequence have little in the way of structure or affection. "To each, his own," or "Live and let live" might be their motto.

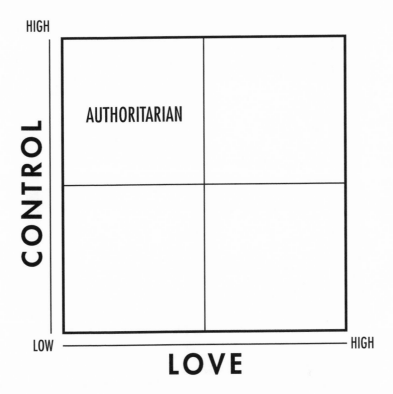

The Authoritarian Family

Moving skyward in terms of control, we now see a family system that is marked by being low on love and affection, but high on control. This is a military-style family. The parents are commanders. Rules are clear and always enforced. Expectations are announced. Discipline and order are obvious to anyone who enters this home. Children understand that they are under the command of their adults and their compliance with adult instructions is mandatory. Everyone knows their responsibilities and fulfills them to avoid the inevitable consequences for breaking the rules. This family demonstrates very little in the way of affection, however. There isn't much warm and fuzzy stuff going on. Hugs and demonstrations of love are seldom seen. If you are lucky, you might get a Valentines Day card in this home, but it probably won't have anything too personal written in it. This is the "Authoritarian" family system. Structure rules.

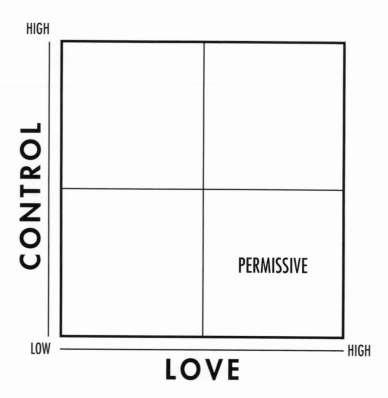

The Permissive Family

In the lower right hand corner we see the Permissive family system. Unlike in the Authoritarian home, in this system children have a tremendous amount of personal freedom and autonomy throughout their lives. Their misbehavior is excused. Talking back to adults is overlooked. Parents in this system feel that they simply cannot tell their children, "No." Missing from their lives is a sense of order, of expected standards. Rules in this home are inconsistent or even non-existent. This child doesn't typically contribute much to the family in terms of chores. Their sacrificial caregivers handle all the heavy work. Instead, the child is repeatedly told how special they truly are. They are surrounded by words and gestures of affirmation, but little is expected of them.

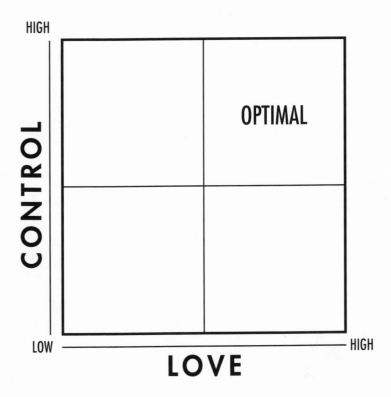

The Optimal Family

The final family system is the Optimal family. It is the ultimate family style and one we would all aspire to establish as parents. This family has the highest levels of both love and control. Standards are set and discipline firmly enforced. The system endeavors to be firm, yet fair. Kids are taught to be responsible and to do their duty before expecting a reward. This family is doubly blessed because it also excels in demonstrating love, warmth, and touch. These high levels of approval give every member a deep sense of security. The order in the home helps prepare them for success in life.

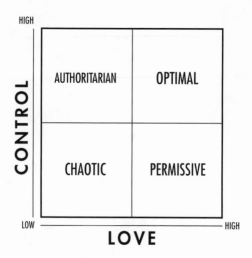

Conclusions

There are two reasons for sharing this diagram. The first is for you to ponder the family style you are operating and to make adjustments if you feel you are off track. This chart helped us in our determination to be an optimal family.

There's another reason we are sharing this with you. Here's a question for you to think about. If high love/high control is the ultimate family style which one is second best?

I was amazed in class to find that according to objective standards of success like children growing up to have lower incidence of divorce, higher employment rates, higher annual income, and a lack of a criminal record, etc., the second best family style of all is...authoritarian. The worst of all was, of course, the chaotic family system. Perhaps surprisingly, the sweet but boundary-free permissive home was the second worst of all types. Food for thought.

We all want to show love and to allow our children to make their own choices as much as they can, but control, discipline and structure seem to be the kind of love that actually build the muscle of champions. So focus on getting the strong stuff established first, then we can all add the softer stuff later. That's parenting in the first half of the parenting workflow, birth through preteens.

 **SECTION FOUR**

The Art of Parenting Children

Parenting is as much an art as it is a discipline. This section is a look at various aspects of "parentcraft," as we might call it. Every trade has its techniques and secrets passed from generation to generation. Here we pass on some of the practical thoughts and discoveries we have made along the way in hopes that they will be as helpful to you as they have been to us.

CHAPTER SEVENTEEN
RAISING BRAVE KIDS

The world is pretty messed up right now. Imagine what it will be like when our children are adults trying to raise children of their own. More than any other generation, our kids need courage.

It takes courage to stand up for your convictions when the vast mob around you hates the fact that you dare to have any convictions at all. It takes courage to face life without your parents. It takes courage to ask a girl to marry you, knowing that it will be an irrevocable decision that will bind you together for life. It takes courage to empty out your savings and mortgage your house so you can open a business of your own.

It takes courage to admit your mistakes and courage to forgive another for theirs and to choose to trust them again. It takes courage to interview for the job you long for, knowing that they will probably reject you in the end. It takes courage to go into battle for your country and courage to face the sounds of the breaking of your back door in the night. Ultimately, it will take all the courage our children can muster to deal with cancer or dementia or whatever comes to claim them in the end, and to face their death alone as we all must.

To survive and thrive in this age of chaotic change, our kids can't just be kept safe. They have to have a core of bravery instilled in them. Bravery will provide the drive they will need to take numerous risks every day in order to seize the life they envision for themselves.

Julia taking a leap.

Andrew and August, both amazed.

All the kids learning to blow fire.
Thanks Travis for sharing your skills!

The current generation of American youth is the most risk-averse in our nation's history. At 35 many remain afraid to commit to marriage and are still living at home with their parents. How did this happen? In our boomer generation most kids couldn't wait to turn 18 and move into their own lives.

Maybe it has to with the way America has become so lawsuit-crazy. Our government is run by lawyers (China's is run by businessmen, scientists, mathematicians, etc.). The result is that across "the land of the free and the home of the brave," we now have rubberized playgrounds and kids so padded up that they can't even hit the ball. Any form of risk and loss seems too great a price for parents to bear any more. "Be careful!!!" has become the core message and whenever loss or injury does occur the instinctive reaction now seems to be to search for someone to blame--and to sue.

When Sherry and I were kids our mother's right arm was the passenger restraint system in our cars. My brothers and I actually got to lay in the window space behind the back seat and look up at the starry sky above as we drove to Alabama to see our kin. It wasn't safe, for sure, but there was something wonderful about it. We're very happy for the advancements in automobile safety. Airbags are great and seat belts save lives (and we wear them), but every kid really does deserve to ride in the open back of a pickup truck sometime. They'll do well to climb dangerously high trees and jump off cliffs into chilly rivers. They need to get into scuffles without someone calling the police. They need to play occasionally in raging thunderstorms and skip school on their birthdays. Can they get hurt doing these things? Yes, but risk and reward will always be bound together throughout this life.

The future belongs to the bold and if we want our children to be bold and free from the bondage of fear and timidity, we need to encourage risk-taking and reward experimental failures. Most of us need to take more risks ourselves.

Weightlessness

We knew we were making progress in becoming a braver family when we took our elementary-aged kids to a pristine river to swim. This was in a wilderness area. It was the first chance the kids ever had to jump off of a bridge. I took the oldest three and we climbed up to the top. There, they surveyed the twenty foot drop into the gently moving waters below.

The water beneath the bridge was about ten feet deep. Sherry was the lifeguard, our latest baby on her hip, standing in shallower waters waist deep about 40 yards downstream to snag them as they floated by if they passed her.

Andrew, the eldest, set his face like a very serious Tarzan and leaped off into space. Kristin was a little more tentative, but after a minute bit her lip and took the leap as well. Nathan was our four-year-old. He was just supposed to watch, but he asked if he could jump. He stood on the edge too long, wanting to jump, but afraid to let go.

After a minute of inner agony he turned his face up to look me in the eye and said, "Dad, would you hold my hands and drop me off this bridge? I can't make myself jump." I wanted to cry. What trust! I dangled his little body in mid-air, half terrified at what I was doing but compelled by my intention to see it through. I knew he could swim well and that this moment would define him forever. I also calculated that I could jump to him in about a second if needed. Still it scared me to death. I can still see it in my mind so clearly. Sherry was screaming, "Don't you do it Chuck Quinley!" but I knew I had to.

I released his hands. Down he hurtled, wind whistling across his board shorts. His silent fall was made all the longer by the tiny size of his body. Sherry and I each held our breath as he slid neatly into the water. As Nathan surfaced, he spun around and locked excited eyes with me up on the bridge. He shouted, "I did it!" Risk and reward, they will always be married.

As I write this, Nathan is on a 2,500 mile hike across snowy mountain passes, lava fields and big bear habitat, walking from Canada to Mexico along the Pacific Crest Trail. He is often alone for days. It will take five months to accomplish, and we are all living the dream with him as he posts his coordinates on a wrist-worn GPS. Jumping leads to hiking, leads to a bold way of living, which leads to all the good stuff.

This was the last photo we took of Nathan before he re-entered the PCT at night and hiked his last month through California, ending at the border of Mexico.

Nathan taking his first step on a 2650 mile journey, the Pacific Crest Trail.

A spirit of bravery is contagious in a bonded family. Andrew and Jacki married and moved to Thailand to do missions work, choosing to have their babies in a local hospital instead of returning to America. Kristin moved alone to Bolivia to work with street kids who had been drug addicts. Jessica and Brooke roamed India for months after working the disease-ridden dying centers of Mother Teresa in Calcutta. Julia, our baby, in her first and only outing, fought an experienced professional Thai kick boxer who was intent on damaging her knee. Bravery is liberating. It opens up a world of possibilities because you have decided not to play it safe all your life.

Here's what we are trying to say to new parents. We know that every impulse inside of you wants to cry out "Be careful!!!!" every time your child attempts something daring, but try –really try– to stop yourself in these moments and instead shout, with conviction, the words they really need to hear, "Be brave!!!"

CHAPTER EIGHTEEN
THE IMPORTANCE OF PLAY

There is much research out there on the effects of TV, iPads and computer games in retarding the creative development of children. As parents, we all know about this so we don't need to say much more about it here. You will either babysit your child with electronics or you won't. It's a matter of conviction. It's sad to watch so many little kids these days with that glazed look in their eyes. They are whiny and irritable, disengaged from the living humans all around them. They crave "the electric device" and when you hand it to them they go deep within it like a heroin addict who just had a fix. I was a guest with a family that had an 18-month-old baby. This child had an iPad in his hands for the entire two days I was with them. The child was oblivious to all that was going on around him and didn't make eye contact with anyone as far as I could tell.

There is creativity in the heart of every child, but electric devices of any kind will snuff it out completely. Play stimulates creativity. Electronic entertainment makes you a lumpy, passive zombie staring at a blue tube. We allowed one hour a day of media while the kids were in school. Keep the visual media drug away from kids for as long as you can. They'll thank you later.

Play is Essential

Play is essential to every healthy life. In the bestselling book, His Needs/Her Needs, William F. Harley, Jr. says that one of the greatest needs in a married man's life is for his wife to be his playmate, not his mother. If a thirty-five-year-old office warrior has need of a playmate, how much more our kids?

The days of young children have always been filled with hours of unstructured play. We even call their friends, "playmates." Though they mature in many other ways, this need never really changes much. Families that are happy and homes that are life-giving have this in common, a light atmosphere and a sense of playful humor.

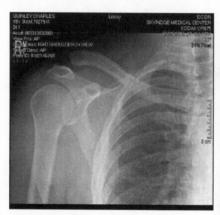

This is what happens sometimes when a 45-year-old dad decides to teach his kids how to ride motocross. The collarbone is still dislocated, but I'd do it again.

Punching through a cold, powerful waterfall.

Being an Active Parent

Don't let yourself become so burdened with the duties of family life, and the rules you need to enforce, that you lose the wellspring of happiness play offers. Lighten up and have some fun together. Be their playmate. Fight the temptation to become a spectator, watching them play. Join in! Go outside and have a water fight. Play ultimate Frisbee. Ride bikes together. Be the parent that stays engaged. Determine that one day you'll be that grandparent who still roller skates with the kids.

Kids want to do more than talk or watch TV together with you. This is your chance to drop twenty pounds and get in better shape. Do things that move your bodies around. In the pool there's Marco Polo. On a trampoline, play crack the egg. Then there are battles of all kinds. Our kids suggested an extreme version of paintball where the boys go shirtless and the girls wear only T-shirts, no pads. After the game everyone celebrated their welts and bruises with great pride.

When our boys were young teens we put up a basketball hoop in the corner of the driveway. Now this was a small driveway, about the size of a free throw lane. We had to open the driveway gates to enlarge the court. The three point line was anywhere past the sidewalk and into the street. Andrew's friends were eager to come over, and we had some glorious battles on that postage-stamp-sized court.

Here's the curious thing. Andrew had a friend whose dad had leased the property adjacent to his own and had built a regulation-sized court with two goals, lights and everything, for his son. The thing was amazing, but hardly used. One night, Sherry, always reading social cues so much better than I did, said, "The reason they would all rather play here is that you play with them. They come in asking where you are and if you will be able to play." That sunk down deep, and I wished I could have back every time I had been too busy to play because of some crushing work project. For those nights when the generations did battle each other on the Quinley court, I will always be grateful. These are warm memories for the kids and for me too.

Too often we take the easy route as parents. We invite a playmate for our child so we don't have to play with them. We let our kids bring friends on vacation so we can have a vacation too and just relax. Sometimes all of that is okay. We are only human, but we need to intentionally (there's that word again) define times when we will go alone as a family and determine to play with them. In times like these, Sherry and I had to remind ourselves to shake off our own fatigue, go the extra mile, and actively engage our children in their world.

It's not hard to find active things to do together. Play "Dance Revolution" on Playstation, or Tennis on the Wii. Take up line dancing. The possibilities are endless. If you are looking for something you can do in the backyard, why not visit http://www.mykidsadventures.com/ and browse their hundreds of ideas.

The Great Outdoors

This generation is losing its touch with the wonder of nature. Urban life is full of distractions that sap the energies needed to replenish our souls. Sunsets, mountaintops and thick forests, these have magical powers to drain stress away and to reconnect us to the earth from which we sprung. All over the globe, nations have set aside wilderness areas for preservation and enjoyment.

America has some of the most beautiful national parks in the world. Most are cheap or even free. If you live in the USA and haven't flown into Denver and driven to Yellowstone and back, we urge you to make this a family goal even if it takes you five years to save enough to do it. There are cheap ways to do anything. You can camp in hammocks. It's comfortable and doesn't cost much. Camp sites cost less than $20 a night. Our family journey has been punctuated with hikes through some of the world's most excellent scenery. We've been swimming in lakes and rivers, and have often been pelted by waterfalls we've climbed and explored. These are simple pleasures everyone can have. We can't overstate the healthy effect of the outdoors in a family's life.

Even if the weather is bad you can still be active in play. Making movies is always fun if the kids are in charge. Give them the camera and turn them loose to create a special video for Mom's birthday or whatever the occasion. Volunteer to be their actor and follow their directions. Our kids' re-enactment of Sherry giving birth to each of them won a family Oscar.

Kristin lay on her back in Sherry's night clothes, screaming as she dropped half a dozen volleyballs and baby dolls off the bench onto the tile floor below.

Beyond the trip, there is the magical thing called an adventure. It has a bit of mystery, danger and the unknown thrown in. There are urban adventures of many kinds as well. Avoid Disney and other canned amusement, and repurpose the $500+ it would have cost you, and instead do something creative and different. For eighteen years, we lived in a city of 13,000,000 people. That's a lot of zeroes. Wilderness adventures weren't going to happen there, but we still had the chance to make a great memory if we'd put in the effort needed.

My sky high birthday celebration.

Playful and Meaningful Birthdays for Everyone

Birthdays are huge in our family, because of the opportunity they give to honor each child and to speak into their lives about their destiny. There are memories just waiting to be created if you take the time to design them and bring them into being.

One year we decided to make scavenger hunts the theme for birthday celebrations. We wanted to make a great birthday memory for each child. This took planning. It started with a visit to the mall to enlist the help of staff working in stores that day. We used the older children to help set things up. Each store was the site of a treat for the celebrant. The store manager would say, "Happy Birthday!" to them at the end and hand them the envelope with their next instruction. We found that the staff were delighted to participate and happy to see a family so intent on surprising each other. After getting new clothes, sweets, music, and a movie, the celebrant came home to find their friends gathered for cake and ice cream.

Each Quinley birthday festival ends with everyone sitting in a circle. One by one, each gives the celebrant a toast, which is either a warm memory, a wish for their next year, or more commonly something about them that they really like. Hearing twenty different people say nice things to you makes your birthday a truly empowering event. Then we all lay hands on the celebrant and pray for their next year.

We do it this way, even if the room is filled with people of varying faiths. This is our tradition and everyone enters in and finds meaning in it. We've had quite a few post-birthday discussions with unplanned guests who were total strangers to us until they happened into the party. They talk about how meaningful and how affirming the birthday celebration was and they always speak about the love they felt. We have always believed that our home, not the church building, was the center of our ministry to the world. Moments like these provide a wonderful opportunity to let your light shine to others who live in darker places.

A child's desire to play with their parents never really stops. Last year we gave our first daughter away in marriage. Two nights before her wedding, all of our tribe spent the night in a big house with the parents and sisters of Ben, our son-to-be. Jessica's main request was that we all play "sardines." Off went the lights as we scurried throughout the unfamiliar rooms of the house looking for great places to hide. Jessica was suffering under the pre-wedding pressures known to every young bride. The antidote for this stress was to play with her family. If you can keep play alive, first in your marriage and then in your family life, you can face any challenge life might throw at you.

CHAPTER NINETEEN
A SPIRITUAL CORE

Sherry and I want to follow the higher callings in life. Both of us have a healthy respect for the brevity of life and want to know that we have left behind us a trail of people whose lives we have enriched in some way. Most importantly, we want to have left a spiritual impact on our children so deep that it will echo for three generations.

It's amazing that the act of union between a husband and wife can lead to the birth of a child made in our own image. The science on this is pretty well understood—DNA, cell division and all. What is absolutely astonishing, however, is the fact that, according to the Bible, our children aren't just little bodies, they have a spiritual core that will live forever.

We believe that inside every human is a spiritual person. This spirit will live on after physical death and is like the God who gave it in many ways. This spirit core is our built-in connection line to Him. Spiritually attuned parents are aware of this and work to nurture their child's spirit as well as their minds.

A child is innately spiritual. Our grandson, August, is less than two-years-old as I write this, and already he can feel the pain of others. He'll moan, "Oh...Oh...Oh" whenever anyone gets injured or is in obvious pain or distress. He also has a heightened connection to nature and spots the Moon at its first appearance every night, though the rest of us may be distracted and miss it entirely. For him, water is a thing that must be felt by the hands and feet. Everything in his world cries out to be tasted and there is nothing in life too small to be commented upon and noted. It's like everything in life is sacred to a child.

There is this great story in the gospels where the mothers of Salem brought their children to Jesus. Some made it through and he held them in his lap. He touched them and invoked his blessing upon their lives. Other mothers saw this and rushed to get their children too. The stern disciples drove them back and told them to go away. Spirituality, for them, was an adult thing that children interrupted.

When Jesus caught sight of this, he rushed to his disciples, furious. It's one of the few times the Bible uses that word to describe Jesus. He took the banished children, began to bless these also and taught the adults around him saying, "If you do not become like these little children yourselves and accept the Kingdom of God like a child you will never enter it." Kids are naturally spiritual.

Christian Spirituality and the Bible

If you ever have hopes of God's Word becoming locked inside your child's heart, then start early. Instill the Bible in their memory. The world will work tirelessly to program your child's mind with its warped value system and as teens they will consume over eight hours of secular media per day on average. While their minds are soft and memorization is an easy thing to do, set up challenges and systems to reward them for memorizing key

I think I've tried everything to make family devotions interesting.

verses from God's word each week. If the Scriptures are hidden in their hearts when they are children they will always be there to guide them in thinking rightly.

The Bible isn't just a book to be memorized. It's God's Word to be obeyed. I heard a teacher say once, "We all choose which parts of the Scripture to ignore." There's a lot of truth to that statement. If Sherry and I truly intended to live in a family that was under God's protection, provision and direction, then we had to take care that we didn't live in a way that was contrary to the heart of God. God has tender concern for the poor, all races, the broken, and those who do not know about Him. He is servant-hearted and humble and He expects the same from us. He hates injustice and the oppression of others due to race, sex, or position in society. He forgives and refuses to hold a grudge. God calls all of us to become like Him.

We planted a house church in Manila when Andrew was in the first grade. One afternoon there was a knock on our front door. We opened it to see a harried mother and a feverish child. She said, "We had my son in the hospital trying to break this fever. I finally told the doctors that I wanted to take care of him at home. What I really wanted was to come by so you could pray for him. I believe that God will heal him if you will just pray."

The child was obviously ill. Sherry and I gathered around to pray for him. As we did, Andrew and Kristin eased up behind us and laid their little hands on the boy's hot brow (kids are very sympathetic to the pain in others). After the mother left I, being a man of great faith, took Andrew and Kristin to the bathroom to wash their hands with disinfectant. Andrew said soberly, as if to prepare me for something bad that might happen, "Dad, I prayed that if he couldn't get well, his sickness would come into me instead." I am still moved at the spiritual insight about sacrificing self for the good of others he had already gained by age six.

Kids "get it" without books, seminars or classes. The idea that the spiritual journey is primarily an educational matter is an entirely modern notion, as though the spiritual life comes from taking a course about being spiritual. Kid's pick up God's revelations through real life situations. This is how God has always spoken to humans. God meets us in life and sends an impulse to our spirit to do something. We either do it or we resist the impulse till it goes away.

Hearing and Obeying the Voice

Adults often admit to carrying constant feelings of guilt. No one should live under guilt. To correct this, counselors might teach them to reject these thoughts of guilt. I wonder if we would all be happier and more guilt-free if as children we were simply taught to obey the little voice. What if all parents keyed on the universal experience of hearing that inner voice and celebrated each time their kids followed what it asked of them?

If we just did whatever the good inner voice of God in our spirit told us to do there would be a lot less to feel guilty about. All kids, like all adults, hear this voice. With encouragement, they can learn to live guided by the Spirit.

Regifting

One Christmas Jessica received lots of wonderful presents from her grandparents, siblings, friends, and from Sherry and me. Much thought went into selecting gifts perfect for her. She was grateful, but looked at the growing pile around her with a thoughtful expression on her face.

A few hours later, we found her happily organizing her gifts. She planned to re-gift them to less-fortunate children later that Christmas day. I still remember the conflicting emotions Sherry and I had to deal with over this. Would it seem ungrateful to the givers for her to give it all away? No matter, the voice in Jessica had spoken and she was filled with happiness at the thought of obeying it.

I wish I could say that we swept her up in our arms, celebrating her purity of heart and her freedom from material things. We should have rushed to help her load the things in the car and immediately have driven her around town to bless others. Instead, we compromised. We allowed her to give a certain amount away, but made her keep much more than she wanted (or needed, to be truthful). I wish I had it to do over again. My heart clearly told me that she was doing the right thing.

CHAPTER TWENTY
SPIRITUALITY & MONEY

Another thing the voice will tell us to do as a family is to give some money away. The ancient Jews gave away something like 25-30% of their overall income through the various requirements of the law like the intentional mis-harvesting of their crops to give the poor a chance to glean the abundant leftovers. The best known Jewish giving system, however, was the tithe, ten percent of one's gross income. Many Christians join their Jewish friends in observing this habit today. Our experience is that once a family decides to participate in God's tithing system for blessing the earth, amazing things will happen financially to them. As many have observed, "God will give it to you, if He can get it through you." More importantly, since giving is the key to everything, becoming a giver will unlock life's opportunities in a way nothing else can.

Our family goal is to give away 25% of our income. We haven't always reached it, but it is the general target we aim for each year. Having lived our adult lives in the developing world we have seen people in need every day. The presence of this standing fund has allowed us to bless the churches where we received our spiritual nurture and feeding. We've been able to help send kids to college, paid for some weddings, and bought medicine for those who couldn't.

We don't share this to toot our own horn. We could have lived on much less and have wasted far too much money on trivial things. We could have done much more for others than we have attempted, yet we have made a difference in some lives simply by being willing to intervene financially. Help only works if it comes when you need it. That's why it has been so important to us to have a giving fund set aside. It has given us the ability to be immediately responsive to needs that God places in front of us.

The consistent pattern of giving money away to help others has had a tremendous impact on our children. For starters, it helped them to develop the concept that they were not poor. A poverty mindset is a crippling thing. Our kids came to know that they had more than enough toys, clothes, books, food—more of everything--and that God had done this intentionally so they could become givers. (If you can buy a book you are already in the top 20 percent of incomes, globally.)

Building on that thought, they came to also accept that they had been empowered by God to be His hands extended to others. This caused them to take the initiative when they saw an opportunity to help. They saw themselves as "the head and not the tail," to quote the prophet Moses. They came to have this thought, " God has given me a great amount of gifts. I will always have all that I need from Him. I am strong and have more than enough. I am blessed to be a blessing to others." Kids who think like this will never be slaves to worry and have the foundation for a secure self-image. The thought came to them through sharing money, beds, food and extra things.

The practice of having our kids join in sacrificing for others gave them an abundance mindset. They became convinced of their power to help others move ahead in their lives without having to ask anything of us as parents. This was evidenced in many practical ways. We'll share a few.

When Andrew graduated High School we gave him a significant check as a celebration gift. He used all of it to buy Nathan a guitar since he could see that Nate was serious about practicing on the entry-level guitar he had. A great guitar would motivate him to go even higher.

When Brooke was 8 years old she was playing at our friend's nearby house and overheard that their helper had been roughed up by her husband in another of his drinking bouts. The woman had come to sleep at her employers' house and was gathering her things to run away from him the next morning. Brooke has always been good with money and had $50 in pesos saved up. In the Philippines this was quite a nest egg, unheard of for a child her age. She opened the secret place in her trunk (their wooden trunks were the only private spaces any of our kids had since so many always slept in the same room) and, without hesitation, took out the fist-full of small bills and wrapped it in a note. She and Julia went to the LaFortune house on their holy mission, prayed for the battered woman's safety and handed her the gift. The helper cried as she saw what was in her hand. It represented her chance for a clean getaway and let her know that God would provide for her in any way necessary, even through little kids.

Years passed, then one day, Julia, our youngest, asked "How much would it cost to send Erica and Jezebel to college when they grow up?" She was a ninth grader at the time, but could already see how important education was at breaking the cycle of poverty. Erica and Jezebel (yep, that's really her name) were the daughters of Gina. She had been our cook before she married Jun and moved to the provinces to start a family with him. In the Philippines, college education is quite reasonable so the answer to her question was, "About $500 each per year, $4,000 to educate them both." She pondered this challenging amount for a moment, then asked her second question, "How do you set up a foundation?" Wow! Big thinking!

Thus was born the "Send Erica and Jezebel to College" fund that Julie set up and donates into each month. Jezebel will enter her first year in college soon, sent there by the savings and fund-raising of a nineteen-year-old who is committed to changing her life.

Spirituality and The Ministry of Hospitality

The spiritual path invites every family to share their home, food and beds with others. We wanted to become an open home for kids in the neighborhood and for young people who needed a place to live for a few months. Being the house of choice for our children's friends will cost you some money. For us it meant buying a trampoline, extra toys, soccer balls and a basketball hoop. It meant having snacks and fruit available for their friends and cooking a little extra every night just in case one of them wanted to stay for dinner.

This allowed us to really get to know our children's friends and to have input in their lives. Kids, of course, are all-too-happy to tell you the truth about what goes on in their family so we got to know more about our neighbors than they might have wanted. For some of these children, our home became their calm oasis, a place they could run to and find shelter from the chaos of their own family. It was also the first time many of them had ever received intentional, focused attention from an adult. They clung to us.

All of this also had a profound impact on the spiritual development of our children. At night, during family devotions, our kids would take turns praying for their friends and their families. They might have been only five years old themselves, but they were already seeing themselves as missionaries and it was rewarding to see their determination to help their friends come to know the Lord.

We gradually expanded our interactions to include the parents and siblings of the kids who hung out in our home. Friday night worked well as a time to schedule families to share a meal at our house. Meeting people in your home is so much more powerful than meeting them in a restaurant. In your house, you can have real conversations and your guests will have the eye-opening experience of stepping inside a Christ-following home.

Ironically, spending all this time and money on others didn't impoverish us. God always paid the bills somehow. We saw many people come to Christ this way and it helped us to live the kind of "family on a mission" life we had always envisioned. Every family has a goal for itself, whether stated or unstated. We just wanted ours to make a difference.

CHAPTER TWENTY-ONE
THE LAW OF FIRST ENCOUNTERS

If every time you opened any door to your house you got hit in the face with a bucket of cold water, it wouldn't take long before you would begin to delay coming home at all, dreading the assault you would inevitably face. We don't usually hit our family members in the face with water, but if we aren't careful we can get into the bad habit of dumping our pent-up emotions on them in much the same way.

In the first year of our marriage, we had many situations sort of like this: I would drop Sherry somewhere and she would say she was going to run into a store and be back in five minutes so I'd wait in the car. Well, you know how that goes. Forty-five minutes later she would return with either a bunch of big bags and the story of a sale, or with few bags and the story of running into a friend who needed to talk.

This usually led to an exchange, followed by a tense quiet that lasted for about six hours and made our stomach churn. Marriage can bring out such intense emotions. Finally I realized that although I couldn't get back the 45 minutes I had sat waiting, I didn't have to lose the rest of the day because of the way I vented my emotions. We both agreed to a new policy called "the law of first encounters" and it has saved us so many needless arguments through the years.

What usually happened before was that as Sherry entered the car she was greeted by, "You said five minutes. It's been an hour!" and the day would be ruined. What we both learned to do in situations like that was to agree that all of our first moments of greeting after being apart would be pleasant, even if we needed to discuss something a bit delicate later.

So in the same example, every time I managed to be "good Chuck" I would simply say, "Hey Baby!" when she opened the door. She would immediately explain, often justifiably, what had happened to delay her without my jumping to conclusions and dumping on her that bucket of cold water we mentioned before. Day saved. (Eventually, I also learned to always carry a book with me in case I had to wait.)

How does this law work in a family on a normal day? Well, it means that we don't greet our fourth grader with, "You left the milk out again," when she comes skipping happily into the house after school. We also don't berate her for anything she has done wrong when she and her friends enter the house together. Everyone in our family gets a sweet welcome every morning and any time we haven't seen them for even an hour. Families that live by the law of first encounters determine that they will make their encounters soft, sweet and positive.

Who doesn't want to come home to hear a child happily call out, "Momma!!!" What husband wouldn't love to slide in the seat at a restaurant and hear his wife say in front of everyone, "I've been looking forward to seeing you again all day." The power of life and death is in the tongue. We can decide to use it to lighten the loads of others and to help everyone in our home feel wanted and cherished.

But I'm Tired

For much of our lives I have had two jobs. To make things worse, in Manila I had a minimum three-hour daily commute. I can't describe how exhausted I was at times. I always did my best to be home in time for our family meal at night, though I once fell asleep within twenty feet of reaching our driveway. I could feel it coming and quickly pulled over and put it in park. I woke up twenty minutes later. I just tell that to say that if your work life is exhausting I know what that feels like. I was tired. That was my burden to bear, but it wasn't my kids'.

They were waiting inside that door for me to come home so we could play or swim or at least interact. The last thing they needed was for me to enter the house like Frankenstein shuffling one foot in front of the other, groaning about how tired I was. So I would stop one block from home and sit in the car for a minute or two giving myself a pep talk. I knew that Sherry had been homeschooling three of our kids that day. She had also been making sure the clothes were washed, the house cleaned and food made ready for dinner. She was as tired as I was. I knew that I needed to sweep her off her feet with a great kiss and a hug and then do the same with my kids. Somehow that quiet moment in the car was enough to refuel me so I could bring up some energy and enter my house with a happy greeting for everyone.

Sherry had to prepare her mind in much the same way. She knew about my load and was considerate of how tired I would be. She needed a break from watching babies and would need me to help distract the kids so she could attend to other things on her unfinished to-do list. She knew, however, that all these things could wait fifteen minutes longer. She learned that she could choose to greet me warmly and to sit and chat for a few minutes while I decompressed and the kids climbed all over me. It made home a place I wanted to come to, a sanctuary, not a bucket of water experience at all. After a few minutes I was reintegrated into the day's family flow and could help her carry the load she'd been dealing with alone all day.

Mom Sets the Tone

Someone has to set the tone for a family. Tone is that unseen delicate perception that makes things either sweet or bitter in a family. Complaining, nagging, blaming, second-guessing, these are relational toxins that can hang in the air like a permanent atmosphere. The good news is that one person can improve the general tone in a household. Sherry says that this responsibility lies with the wife.

The word "wife" means "weaver." It's very apt. A wife takes the physical spaces of the home, the family schedule of activities, the food they will eat, the clothes they will wear, the calendar, their outside social interactions and even the music that is played in the house. Then she weaves all of these into one coherent life for her family. It's an amazing skill and you can spot a family whose weaver has mastered the required skills.

Sherry says that moms are in charge of setting the tone for proper interpersonal exchanges in a family. Because every child is different, even the technique of how to wake them up in the morning needs to be carefully considered and chosen according to temperament. My idea of a good morning wake up was to whip up the volume on Jerry Lee Lewis' "Great Balls of Fire" and try to hype everyone up for the day by dancing around the house. It actually worked the first few times but had definitely lost its appeal by the time the second set of three were born.

I was slow to grasp the fact that some of my ways actually set off a grumpy spirit in a child that wasn't necessarily rebellion. They just needed some peace and quiet in the morning. Some kids loved slow tickles. Others liked music. Nathan rubbed his sleepy eyes for a while, then slipped catlike to the floor and got ready in silence. Kristin requested, "Please don't wake me with kisses. It's too early for that." Brooke, well, we just didn't speak to her very much in the mornings and didn't hold her grumpiness against her. She took a few hours to warm up to her days.

The law of first encounters says that we try to help everyone enter the first moments of their new day in a way that has a positive result for them, and insure that our initial encounters throughout are upbeat and pleasurable.

Celebrating after Kristin found
and bought her first car.

CHAPTER TWENTY-TWO
THE MOST POWERFUL TEACHER

More than any formal means of indoctrination, the stories we tell transmit our heart's values and our worldview to our children. Are people generally good or evil? Is any race better than another? Why are some people so poor? Are the rich to be envied, pitied or hated? Is the government to be respected? Can police be trusted? Should I fight in wars? Can girls trust boys? Is there anything unique and special about our family? The answer to all these questions is contained in the stories we choose to tell our children and in the decision of which stories we refuse to tell.

The most gripping illustration we've experienced about the power of story came from a relationship we developed with a young man from Rwanda who had been present during the month-long genocide when over one million people were savagely murdered by their neighbors. Here is his story retold:

> "One afternoon my uncles all gathered at my house. Every one of them had a machete. They talked for a while, then walked next door to my playmate's house. His family screamed and ran into their house. When my uncles started to surround the house the family ran out the door and climbed up the tall tree we always played in. I watched my uncles surround the tree and talk to them all afternoon until one member of the family climbed down. They immediately killed them with the machete. One by one, the rest of the family followed until they were all laying in a heap at the base of the tree. I asked them why they did that to my friends and they said it was because they were evil Tutsis. Tutsis had murdered the Hutus long ago so we were paying them back.

The strange thing was that many of us didn't even know what tribe we were until the government made us get national ID cards a year earlier and we had had to research our tribe. No Hutu I knew had ever been abused by a Tutsi, nor had our parents. It happened one hundred years ago. Our grandparents and parents had kept the hatred alive, though, by telling us the stories over and over again."

Nothing communicates your family values more than your stories. Family storytelling is huge, especially in a child's elementary and middle school years.

Curating A Library of Family Stories

While the cement was still wet and our children's worldview was in the process of being formulated, we wanted to seize the opportunity to intentionally tell and retell a carefully selected anthology of family miracle stories, funny stories, cautionary tales, heroic legends and even the dark drama of our losses and of lessons we learned the hard way. One story I told my children was about my dad. Dad has always been to me a mountain of a man and the standard of morality and ethics. He set the plumb line in our family and enforced right standards without fail.

In this particular story, Dad had come home from the office early, still in his suit, and we had travelled to an inconveniently-distant town for the district little league baseball championships featuring my little brother, Mike. He was chosen to be on the All Star team, coached by Bill Durden. Inning after inning we waited for Mike to take to the field, but it didn't happen. Dad tried a friendly approach with the coach, suggesting that he give Mike a chance in the closely-contested game. In the end, since this was the championship and not regular season play, Bill focused on winning, not on playing everyone, and Mike never got his chance to hit that winning run we knew he had in him. It was unfair and my dad told him so after the game with a bit of emotion.

After that, we walked silently to the car and drove to the nearest Shoney's Big Boy restaurant where the smell of grilled burgers lifted our mood and restored the normal family chatter. Dad was mostly silent through our meal. Then he got up, walked to the cash register and picked up their phone.

This was in the pre-cell phone days when the only way to call someone was to wait till they were at home or work, call directory assistance and find their number, then ring them up. Dad made a call using the phone by the cash register. I was puzzled. Mom said calmly, "Your father is calling Bill Durden to apologize to him." I couldn't believe it. Dad came back to the table and told us why and where he had been wrong and that he had, indeed, apologized to Bill. I was proud of my dad and from his example I knew just what to do whenever I did something that strained a relationship with a friend. No books, lectures, or seminars needed. Stories can do it all.

Tell of Your Failures as Well as Your Successes

Figuratively at least, every family has a few skeletons buried in the back yard if you just know where to dig. Failures, sins, scandals, and intrigues are the legacy of even the most exemplary people. For the most part, we like to keep these embarrassing revelations buried and forgotten.

I trust the Bible's historic accounts, partly because of the sins that are admitted to in the stories of its heroes. Noah got drunk and was possibly molested by his own son. Abraham wimped out and would have let a powerful king sleep with his wife if God hadn't intervened to stop it. David murdered his most loyal follower, stole his wife, and on it goes.

The book of Mark is Peter's telling of the story of Jesus and his life with the apostles. It is so compelling that Peter's account of the betrayal and suffering of Jesus includes so much detail about his own cowardice and how he denied even knowing the Lord three times in a row and that he went out and wept bitterly. Imagine the affect of that story when Peter, himself, head of Christ's church, told it in public to adoring crowds. He didn't edit out his own failures.

As Mark Driscoll has reminded us, we all have to decide whether we want to have a personal legend or a testimony. In our personal legend we edit the story so that we are always the hero. Our goal is to bring glory to us for our accomplishments. Most autobiographies of famous people read like that. A testimony is radically different. In a testimony, God is the hero and we are the illustration of how wonderful He is. A testimony brings glory to God for His greatness and for the way He expresses his love to us over and over in our lives. Our kids need to hear our testimony more than they need to believe our edited version of our legendary history.

Peter was content to give Jesus the glory for loving him back after his failure. He freely told his cautionary tale to warn the next generation of Jesus-followers who were soon to be persecuted by the full power of Rome. He himself died soon, also on a cross, crucified upside down. He had a second chance to deny the Lord and escape this awful torture, but this time he proved completely loyal to his Lord and his friend. His story is a double win.

The Teachable Moment

You never know when a situational story will arise. Something happens and you sometimes have to decide whether to tell a story about it or hold it back. In general, we'd advise you to go for it. There is nothing more powerful than "the teachable moment" when a child asks a question in a quiet block of time and the world stands still. If we don't maximize these opportunities they will evaporate in seconds.

One of my fathering traditions is to shave our daughters' legs the first few times till they can do it without cutting themselves to pieces. I remember the day when, after months of Jessica's persistence, Sherry and I decided that it would be OK for her to start shaving. Her little sisters, Brooke and Julia, crowded around us in the tiny bathroom, excited to watch. As I lathered and started to carefully shave Jessica's right leg, Brooke asked oh-so-casually, "Dad, where do babies come from?" (She's always had an instinct for the killer question to ask in any situation.)

I paused for a minute and calculated their age. Pretty young. I do believe, however, in the power of the teachable moment, so I took a deep breath and we talked about it for the next ten minutes in a question and answer session I wish I had on tape. I knew I needed to tell Sherry about our conversation that night before we slept. I didn't get the chance. Brooke couldn't wait to share her amazing new discovery with her even-younger cousins when they came to dinner that night. You know how a good story travels.

Story Bombs

Then there is the story bomb. A story bomb is a sensitive story that goes off unexpectedly and harms someone in its telling. In his book, To Be Told, Dan Allender tells his memory of the ultimate story bomb.

> *My story begins when I was nineteen years of age. I was looking through a box of photos stored in my mom's closet, and I found a family portrait. It was a picture of my mom, a young boy (me) of about three, and a man I'd never met. The look of his face haunted me...."Who is that man?" I asked....She replied, "It is your father" ...Standing in the kitchen with my mother, I fell and hit within a millisecond, but it has taken me three decades to finally name what that means. I pointed to the man my mother identified as my father. "You mean the man sleeping upstairs?" She said, "No, he is your stepfather. The man in the picture is your biological father....In an instant my life had become both a farce and a great mystery to me."*
> *(p.12f)*

Our experience as pastors would say that a parent needs to tell identity-altering stories like this early in a child's life. Every relationship is founded on trust, so how can we hope to build an even deeper relationship with our teens (absolutely essential for success in this stage of parenting) if they find out we have been hiding the truth, or even outright lying to them, for all of their lives. (Allendar's book, by the way, is about interpreting our life's story, and it is truly remarkable.)

Guiding Younger Siblings Through Stories

Our eldest daughter, Kristin, was the first of our four girls to experience High School, mean girls, cute boys, college and the search to know her calling and to find Mr. Right. She has a bit of gypsy in her and has lived in the Philippines, Bolivia, South Korea, China and recently in Portland, Oregon, USA.

Kristin has always taken to heart the role of being the big sister. She has a parental love and protectiveness toward all her sisters. As a consequence, she made the decision to be totally transparent with them about everything she has ever done. Positive or negative, she shared her experience of life freely so her little ones would know where the good things are and what mistakes they must avoid.

We worried a bit about what some of this information might do in the minds of her youngest sisters and told her that what she had decided to do was great, as long as she would wait to tell certain things till the situation warranted it, versus having an all-girls-circle night where she told all things at once.

Our girls would say today that Kristin's openness made them more open too and set the tone of transparency as the rule between them. (If you can't be honest with your own sister who can you be honest with?) The devil does his work in the darkness, so we think that the fewer secrets within a family, the better. Discretion, however, is just common sense. Tell stories at the right time and the impact will be felt at the deepest levels.

Stories Young Kids Need to Hear

Kids need to hear stories about their uniqueness and their giftedness. In the first grade, my teacher, Mrs. Janice Grenade, wrote home on my progress report, "Chuck is a natural leader." My mom made sure I heard that story a few times in my childhood, told in front of others, and it definitely contributed to my image of myself as being a leader.

Kids should hear the stories about them being spared. It is important that they have an awareness that God has created them for a purpose and that already He is holding them securely in His hands. They need not fear in this life because they are, in those famous words, "immortal until God is finished with them."

Tell them the stories of good things they have done and what these things reveal about them. Catch 'em doing something right and talk about it forever, especially to others in their presence.

Some stories are situational and are called forth in response to an experience your child is facing at a particular point in his or her life. We might say something like, "I had this teacher once, that just didn't like me, just like your teacher is doing to you. It was like he prejudged me as a type of person that was going to give him trouble, and that wasn't me at all. He didn't even take the time to know me." It's probably best to just stop where this one stopped above. These stories don't have to end with you telling how you conquered your mountain. The idea is to get your child to open up and to see you as a human, not just their authority figure. This grows more important as your child approaches their teens.

Conclusion

Stories are simple, but powerful things. They go beyond our intellect and reason and into the depths of our soul, attaching themselves to our emotions and forming much of the framework behind our value system. As parents we decided to use the power of story intentionally for the benefit of our tribe.

EXERCISE

Make a list of the best stories you have in your family memory banks. Think of important stories you need to reinforce in the lives of your children. Finally, create a high-quality media collection of storybooks, novels, biographies and videos that you want to make sure find their way into your children's hearts and minds before they enter High School.

The Beginning of the End of Control

The control stage (the left side of the diagram) might sound like a big heavy thing, but it really doesn't last long. Focus on establishing total control and authority over your child from birth until they lose their front teeth. Then things begin to change ever-so-gradually and a long period of slowly-declining control begins.

This section deals with the middle point in this process and will help you navigate the changes you'll need to make in your relationship as your child enters their teen years. If you have the faith, courage and humility to make these changes your child will welcome and even value your continued participation in their young adult life.

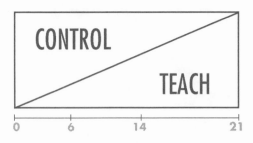

CHAPTER TWENTY-THREE
HOW TO KEEP YOUR CHILDREN FROM BREAKING FREE

The feeling that we are losing control of our children accelerates when they leave our constant, shaping presence and go to an environment called "school." In this place they will be tested in many ways and experience great successes and some failures too. Not to worry, the grace of failure is valuable and they will probably learn more from it than anything else (as long as they analyze the failure).

In elementary school your child will begin accelerated intellectual and academic development, tracked by being graded for the first time in their lives. Grades are an imposed system just to have something to use as a measuring stick and an institutional form of control. The real development going on inside your child during this period comes from the swirling assortment of new personalities all around your children. Most of their new adult authorities you will not even know. What they tell your children, you will not hear. Your kids will also make friends. Some will be sent by God. Others will come to tempt or tease your child. If you have used your first six years to instill a strong foundation of values and character, your child will be up to the test.

During this stage your child will start to grow up and slowly away from your authority. A small seed of independence will take root in the core of their heart and their ultimate adult life will begin to reveal itself gradually as they mature week by week. We need to celebrate this because it is from God and is the force that will cause them to prefer the challenge of an independent adult life to stagnating comfortably in the family nest forever.

Our advice is that you maintain as much control as you can for as long as you can throughout the first ten years of your child's life. During adolescence, the child's craving for independence will grow exponentially and you will need to gradually loosen the reins. If, when they were ten years old you already routinely let them go wherever they wanted and sleep over with friends all weekend, you will have little reward to give them later.

Although our true power of control over our child weakens year by year, it is still the crucial securing factor keeping them grounded to the values we have been drilling into them. Their connection to us (not to their friends) is what holds them to a noble standard of ethical and healthy living. We've had our kids tell us before to please say that they couldn't go to a certain party so they could use us as their excuse. They knew that the proposed party was a scene they didn't want to be part of. They admitted that it was an

unhealthy invitation, but didn't have the strength to stand up against the pressure of peers on their own yet. Kids need us to hold that line for them although it is a complicated matter requiring skill and self-control on our part.

It never gets any easier to say goodbye to them at the airport.

The thing you will want to avoid with early teens is the severing of your intimate heart-connection with them. Some kids simply break away from their parents emotionally. They create as much distance as they can from their parents and the authority they represent. Don't accept this as inevitable. Your children will certainly move increasingly into an independent young adult life but you can definitely go on that journey with them.

Much of the outcome, frankly, depends on you as a parent and on the amount of finesse you are willing to develop in the increasingly complex relationship between you. On the one hand, you don't want to be a needy parent, chasing after your child's affection. Children have to respect you as a person. You need a life of your own as a couple and as a healthy adult who is more than just a parent. Don't act desperate for their affection. Clingy mothers are gross. On the other side, you also can't go head-to-head in battle with them, pulling and pushing and reminding them of your authority every time the two of you talk. There is a middle way and the parent who finds it will keep their child connected to them even as they wrestle with their child's God-given urge to explore the world beyond the home that beckons to them incessantly.

It's Like Deep Sea Fishing

Landing a prize marlin or swordfish in the open seas takes hours, sometimes even a whole day. The hook is firmly set when the massive fish takes the bait and the line becomes as taut as piano wire. If all you do is lock down and pull in with all your might, the fish will pull against you, snap the line, and your connection to your prize will be lost. (Some parents lose touch with their children in preteen years from just this approach. The child then develops an entirely separate, secret life, and may even begin to lose the emotional bond they felt toward their parents up to that point.)

To avoid this disaster, the fishing reel has a feature on it, called "drag." Drag allows you to set a limit just on the inside of the breaking strength of the line. Let's say, for example, that you have hooked a 200 pound fish on 100 pound strength line. In a face off of sheer strength, the fish wins, snaps the line and runs away from you. Drag allows you to set the mechanism to yield to the fish when it pulls at, say, 80 pounds pressure. The fish pulls and you hold firmly, but not aggressively. The fish pulls and wins a bit, but at a cost to the amount of energy it spends in the battle. When the marlin stops pulling to rest a bit, you reel in the lost line and go back to the point you were at in the beginning. The fish pulls again and you yield a little bit again, but hold firmly overall. The situation repeats itself until the fish is just too tired to pull away any more.

Parenting teens and preteens is a bit like that. Hold tight. Don't make it a "battle to the death" between them and you. But, please don't let go of the tight line that connects the two of you, even if the contest exhausts you.

I had teen friends who went so much farther into life-crippling trouble than they ever would have, simply because their parents gave up in the early stages of their teen battles and let them run free. Just hold on. It won't last forever. Adolescents will test the boundaries. It is their nature to always fight for more liberty. In general, give ground slowly, but you will have to give ground over time if you want to keep them connected to you. Just give ground on your own terms and as a reward for their staying in a posture of voluntary submission to your loving authority.

Do You Know Where Your Child is?

When I was a teen, there was this public service announcement on TV every night that said, "It's ten o'clock. Do you know where your child is?" This week I saw a modernized version on a billboard: "It's 3PM. Do you know where your child is?" Unsupervised time away from competent adults is dangerous time for children at any age. Enter into these situations with great caution. Once you go there you can't come back easily. It's very difficult, if not impossible, to suddenly rein in a 15-year-old girl who has been free for the last six years just because her parents have finally noticed that she has breasts and are afraid of the consequences of her independence.

Childhood development is a one-way street and the parenting process needs to follow the direction of that traffic flow. Firmly establish absolute control over your small children, then prepare yourself for the interim period of declining control that will last from around ages six to sixteen.

Like it or not, you are losing control from the time your child starts school. This will continue throughout their years with you until they finally kiss you goodbye and enter their adult life. Don't panic. You are still their spiritual authority, but yours will ultimately have to become a kind of control that they decide to grant you willingly, versus one you can force upon them.

By this middle stage in the parenting journey, you should have earned their respect as a firm, but fair, parent whose words and actions have always been motivated by love for them. They will choose to show you respect and will generally abide by your house rules in a broad sense though they may test the system a bit from time to time.

CHAPTER TWENTY-FOUR
THE TIPPING POINT, AGE 14

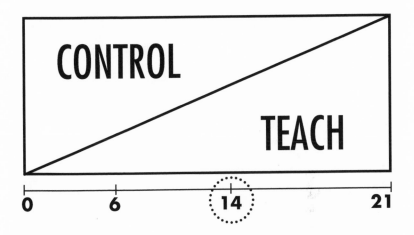

Every child develops at a different pace, but the most important year of a child's later development seems to be age fourteen. It's something of a tipping point year, the time when the balance of power shifts perceptibly from their parents to a kind of unsteady equilibrium where things are clearly in motion away from the old ways, but nothing seems to be clearly decided about where it will all end.

Think of this year as a see-saw experience. For all their lives they have been standing on one end and you, the parents, have been on the other end. From their earliest memories you outweighed them so much that they could never budge the balance an inch. As a small child, they could jump on it with all their might but it remained as firm as if it were cemented to the ground. Now, however, things have started to change. Their body has grown closer to yours in size and since they were about ten years old they have felt increasing movement when they put pressure on their end of the board. At fourteen, in a dramatic turn of events, your end suddenly lifts off the ground and hovers at the mid-point. This is scary to both parties on this see-saw, but it is also exhilarating. Their young heart yearns for freedom and independence and this is the first clear sign that things are changing permanently in their favor. They can move you now. They are starting to have power over their own life.

Sherry and I have pretty much concluded that year 14 decides how much tension and grief everyone will experience for the rest of a child's teenage years. In this year, a child decides what kind of teen they are going to be. Around this time, they often change schools, choose a new peer group and dress in a new style. They also decide what kind of attitude they are going to put on every day. Helping a child set a healthy course through the age 14 transition is one of the most important tasks in parenting.

This is also the year when parents have a transition of their own to manage. The tipping of the see-saw signals our need to transition from being top-dog to encouraging coach for our teenagers. If we don't begin the transition they can't either, so we both waste the next six years wrestling over who is in control. Don't miss the chance to remain a welcomed partner in your child's wonder years of early adulthood. Teen years can be so amazing if both parties will cooperate with the inevitable process.

Some parents' strained efforts to maintain a lifetime role of "enforcer of law and order" actually distract their child from doing the crucial work of getting prepared to deal with the coming challenges of their own tumultuous young adult life. They have to deal with their greatest season of temptations, insecurities, and opportunities for development. Teens will often set the course of their entire adult lives by the attitude and general pattern of choices they internalize in their earliest teen years. This is a season when they really need our help, but not in the way we helped protect and train them before.

Knowing When to Back Off

Part of the art of parenting in those early teen years is knowing when to back off. I think moms have a special problem with getting this right. Not just any mom, mind you. Some moms are already cutting the cord well before their child has any desire for it. Other moms though are what we might call "SuperMoms." These are diligent women of power and persuasion. They are "she-bears" and woe to anyone who gets between her and her cubs! Sherry is like that.

I fell in love with Sherry partly because her highest ambition in life was to be a world-class mother. As such, Sherry has studied all of her children like a scientist from the day they were born. She is watchful and engaged with all her children. (Even now, she checks in with every one of our scattered kids daily to see how they are doing.)

Andrew, our eldest, had a rocky entry into adolescence. He was the firstborn son, of a firstborn son, of a firstborn son, so there was lots of alpha male in him. Teenage hormones, of course, are like drugs that intensify every feeling. Andrew began to change. He both asserted himself and withdrew from us at the same time. Sherry's initial response was to meet intensity with intensity. She's a strong woman and was gearing up to dig and push and question him in response to his changes. I remembered my own rocky teen experience, much worse than his, and could see on the horizon the same kind of pain I and my good parents had gone through for many years.

I told her, "Sherry, you have to back off and give him some space." That was counter-intuitive. Her normal wiring was to "engage the bull." I told her, "Just stay close and be his comfort and his friend. He'll rage and push, but not forever. If we confront him too aggressively, these things will escalate and there will be pain we could have avoided." She knew I spoke from experience and resolved to take that course.

It wasn't easy and I sometimes had to be the "bad cop," leaving her to be the "good cop," but we got through those years with no permanent damage on either side.

The point is that teen years are the years of permission-based intimacy between you and your child. We can't just barge in and demand closeness. Sometimes, though we reach out to them, they won't invite us in. Don't give up. Keep making the overtures. Show up every day to love and touch and talk. When they begin to talk about anything just be quiet. I literally bit my tongue so many times, just holding it still with my teeth and telling myself, "Just listen to them," so I wouldn't enter into reasoning or correcting them and lose the moment we were having. Whenever a teen opens up and talks with you is a magic moment. Give them your undivided attention and don't make them feel they are interrupting you from something you would rather be doing.

If nothing else happens in these early adolescent years, make sure they remember later all the times you reached out to them and that you worked diligently to develop a deeper walk with them.

This important fourteenth year is driven by the child's need to gain mastery in a world of constant, disruptive social change. Like it or not, the rodeo gate before them is about to swing open at any moment. Things are going to get very dramatic for them, and you as a parent need to switch gears now to get them firmly anchored in their saddle with an adult skill-set that will enable them to stay on when life bucks wildly now and in the future. Navigate through age 14 well and enjoy the ride throughout the remainder of their teen years.

CHAPTER TWENTY-FIVE
GATHERING UP YOUR PONY

If control is the only parenting tool you have, then you'll be in deep trouble by the time your child reaches fourteen. You're in a losing position that's only going to get worse with time. You have to represent more to your adolescent child than some distant, disapproving authority.

Thank God we have a second, more powerful tool! This one, unlike control, has no expiration date on it. You can use it for the rest of your life as the parent of adults and the grandparent of the next generation. We're talking about the role of teacher and coach and this, dear friend, is the key to enjoying raising teens. Successful parents shift roles gradually from power-based control to permission-based teaching and coaching as their children progress through their teen years and into adulthood.

Some parents never make this shift. As "one trick ponies" who think their only job is control, they have constant battles throughout their child's teens. In this case, the poor child either rages against the parental wall or, more likely, develops an entirely hidden life. They are polite to their parents but they lie constantly and create a world of alibi's so they can go off with their friends who alone know the truth about them. This approach robs the whole family of the opportunity to celebrate the child's increasing independence and usually leaves emotional scars on child and parent that mar their relationship.

Accept that your controls are short-lived in the life of your teen. It's their life after all.

If you want to continue to play a part in your child's life as they enter their teen years, you will have to change your role but before that, you need to tighten up the relationship that exists between the two of you. Key on this in those interim years between ten and fourteen.

Lessons from the Dressage Ring

For one wonderful year in my otherwise hectic adult life I got to spend quite a lot of time riding horses. Proper English saddle lessons were on my bucket list and, with Sherry's encouragement, I began to go for early morning lessons before joining the lines of commuter traffic. I had a lot to learn and enjoyed the coaching from my Irish instructor. In the end, everyone wants to gallop, right? Moving from trotting to cantering to a full gallop is one of the most exhilarating experiences ever. It's horrifying and exciting all at the same time.

My trainer taught me that as the big horse flexes his muscles and begins to strain to break free into a full run, you often have to "gather him up" first. As the horse becomes excited about the new level of speed and freedom he's about to get, he often overexerts and gets wobbly and out of sync in his stride. The rhythm is off and it just feels awkward. Letting the raging beast run in such a situation predicts potential danger for the horse and yourself as the rider because you are bouncing everywhere and the horse isn't moving its body in a straight line.

Stronger Physical Contact

What you do is to gather him up into your control again, not by stopping his progress, or wheeling in the reins with full force, but through additional contact. As you gently move to the speed of a canter you tighten up your legs as they grip him to increase the contact between the two of you. This is crucial. If the horse moves to a full gallop and you aren't seated deeply enough, you will bounce all over the place and spend more time in the air than on the horse's back. When you do make contact with him it will be this painful crashing onto his back, then bouncing up and back down again. This hurts the horse and gets everyone out of control. You need to gather up the distance between the two of you and make your connection stronger.

Tighter Lines of Communication

Now, you also gently take up any remaining slack in the reins until you have a stronger line of communication and are sure the horse is listening to your messages. Doing this isn't telling him to slow down or that he won't be allowed to run after all. The opposite is happening. The horse, especially if it's a polo pony, knows that this increased contact means that you two are about to really go places together. As the horse firms up its own movement, its stride becomes shorter and tighter. The rhythm of the hooves becomes perfect. Then you ease the reins just the lightest bit, squeeze your legs even more, and your thoroughbred will dial up the speed in an orderly way. Soon, the wind will be whistling in your face. This is the best part of horse riding. Speed with control.

The same thing needs to happen with a child of about ten to fourteen. They see and feel the freedom all around them and begin to pull away from us increasingly. They become more willful and we get bounced around by this and become disconnected from their world. The worst thing for them would be for us to drop the reins with a sigh and say, "I give up! It's your life."

Adolescents have enthusiasm, but not enough control. Their attempts at breaking free are often tinged with anger. This hurts them and you. Just dropping the reins sends them off running wild in their uncoordinated, extremist ways. They will make bad decisions and then your only contacts with them will be painful ones, times when you ride their back about their errors and they attempt to buck you off and run away from you.

None us us want to face this kind of season during our child's teenage years. That's why we adults need to take sure steps to deepen the level of connection and communication between us and our young teen.

Not With Harshness

Please note that we "gather them up" with us, not by issuing harsher new rules but with the same two things that work for horses, increased contact and stronger lines of communication. Bonding. It's the key to everything.

To accomplish a deeper bond with our adolescent kids, Sherry and I knew that we would have to spend more time with each child one-to-one. Saturday dates with dad alone and taking each child with me on an interesting business trip created hours of time to talk uninterrupted. Sherry also took them out on dates and gave whichever one was struggling the most an extra hour at night laying in the bed with them talking in the darkness. Then she came back to me and told me what had been said so I'd know what she knew.

Preteens need more physical contact from you. Boys and girls still need to be wrestled. Its a good time to challenge them physically to compete athletically, to climb mountains and do daring feats. Our girls loved these things too. They need warm affection also, though they may or may not initiate it. We never stopped kissing them on the cheek or the head, even in front of their friends. We just kissed their friends too and they loved us for it.

It was wonderful to have our children choose to give us a warm hug and kiss goodbye even in front of their schoolmates. They didn't care who saw them. They loved Sherry and me the way we loved them and they weren't ashamed to show the level of our affection. This gesture made us to know that they were secure in themselves and that we were staying connected as they ventured farther and farther afield from us and the home into the new world that was calling to them.

CHAPTER TWENTY-SIX
ENTERING THEIR WORLD

As we have said, when our child enters their adolescence, the conditions that have previously given us strong power and control over them pass from us. This doesn't mean that our young teen no longer needs a relationship with us or that we will necessarily lose our influence with them. More than ever, they need to know us, but now in a different and much deeper way. This is a new stage when we begin our life together as adult friends. Most of the work of accomplishing this shift must come from us. In general, we have to go to them and enter their world, in order to bring them into ours. This will require numerous changes in the posture we have taken with them during our season of serving as the enforcer of controls.

Changing the Tone of How We Speak to Them

There are many varieties of tone in human conversation. There is a way you talk to a friend and a way you talk to someone you feel is under you. We have never allowed our kids to speak to us with a tone of contempt in their voice and we held the same standard for ourselves. Our tone was always one of mutual respect, but there is a decided command form appropriate when you are in charge of younger children. You direct them. That's how you keep things moving ahead in an orderly way.

With young kids, most of your sentences are in the imperative form. "Alright guys, wash your hands and come down for dinner!" This might be said cheerfully, but still it's a command and its a normal way to address children. Changing from a controlling parental stance to a collaborative peer-to-peer one meant that Sherry and I needed to adjust the tone we typically used in our communication toward our children as they moved into their mid teens.

Even in times when we had to tell them they couldn't do something they wanted to do, our young teens responded well to parental statements like this:

> "Honey, we want the same thing that you do. We want to see you fully independent, making all of your own decisions. Even beyond that, we want to see you thriving as an adult with a job that excites you, paying your own bills, driving your own car and living in your own place. This next stage in our lives together is the one where we release control as you demonstrate that you are ready to fly solo. You earn the right as you show that you are thinking and acting with a grown-up mind, not a child's. We are excited about helping you master the grown up world and don't ever want to hold you back. This doesn't have to be a frustrating time. We only have a few more years together, and we want to enjoy them with you and have great memories for the rest of our lives. So work with us, ok? Here are our concerns about this thing you want to do...."

Personal Style

Sherry and I recognized a natural generation gap between us and our kids that was only going to grow with time if we didn't address it. For most of their childhood we were in tight control of them, and the relationship was on our terms. We told them what the right kind of music was. We bought their clothes for them and decided what style we liked to see them in. With the approach of adolescence, things had to change. We needed to enter their world and let that world modify our tastes and perceptions.

If Sherry and I have learned anything about parenting teens it is this: the teen years are your chance to build a relationship with them by respectfully entering their world. In their world, they are the experts.

In the 90's the preppy look was in. Sherry loved it. It meant that our kids would look neat and clean. Andrew was about twelve and would rather take a beating than wear Sperry topsiders and a button-down shirt. He wanted baggy jeans and oversized shirts and to look like MC Hammer. He and Sherry wrestled over this. Especially on Sundays, it became a big issue. We were the pastors of a megachurch, after all, and there was something of a spotlight on us. Hip hop had not yet come to Manila and yet Andrew wanted to already wear his own version, far ahead of the wave. In his chosen style, he definitely stood out and it looked horribly sloppy to her. She didn't want people to judge him as a thug or her as a bad mom.

Sherry took it to the Lord and He gave her wisdom through a simple question. "Is this a moral issue?" That one question became our guiding light from then on. We both agreed that wearing baggy pants was not a moral issue. Then we must not treat it as though it were. Sherry read somewhere that the teen years are the years of "choosing your battles and biting your tongue." Give in on non-essentials and hold a line of steel on areas that are truly moral in nature. Doing this correctly required both us and the kids to commit to recognize moral from non-moral issues.

We set certain ages as times when kids could look forward to making higher-impact decisions about their personal style, like coloring their hair, shaving it off completely (two girls did it—once) and piercing their ears, noses or belly buttons. Tattoos had to wait till they were over 18. The only rule we had for them was "You can dress cool, but you can't act bad." That is, boys can have long hair and everyone could pretty much wear the clothes they liked, but they couldn't act hard and mean and take on this whole dark persona. Because we used the preschool years to help them accept that we were the adults God had placed in their lives to guide them and because we had all of them under control by age six, they were just grateful to have gained the liberty to choose their own personal style at all. It was a fun journey with lots of experimentation and crazy phases.

CHAPTER TWENTY-SEVEN
MOM, CAN I DRESS YOU?

Once our early teens had mastered their own style, they turned their attention on ours. Kristin came to Sherry sweetly one day and asked with total sincerity, "Mom, can I dress you?" "Why? What's wrong with my clothes?" Sherry replied. With polite hesitation Kristin replied, "Well, you just need a little help. So, can I pick out your clothes?"

Sherry realized what a special opportunity this was for both of them, and replied, "Just don't make me look like I'm trying to be a teenager." With that Kristin began meeting with the other kids to decide what style Sherry would look the best in. I was the next target for updating. Their changes were gradual at first so we could become comfortable with our new looks. It was amazing to see how sensitive they were to what we would be feeling at having our own personal style dictated by someone else (they had lived it for many years).

Since then, their word on our clothes is law (and we can't believe how 'missionary' we looked in our old photos). If the kids say, "That's totally out," there's no reason to check to see whether GQ agrees. Kids know trends and feel them before marketers begin to make their inevitable changes.

Two important things came out of this experiment. First, we began to feel better about ourselves because we felt younger inside. More importantly, we had begun to connect with our children on a personal level, beyond the typical "I-thou" parental boundaries. We came to know each other as individuals, not just according to our established roles.

Deeper Than Clothing

Clothing is just the beginning of the journey. The next level comes as you really get to know their friends. Serious parents are always concerned to know about their kids' friends for security reasons. That's normal, but that's not what we are talking about here. We mean that to know your teen as a friend you have to join their friendship circle and come to know and appreciate their friends the same way they do. That means hanging out and logging a respectable amount of time with their friends.

You might think that your kids wouldn't want you to know their friends, but, then again, you might be surprised. The secret is to stop the Inquisition. Just accept that their friends, like yours, have issues they are trying to deal with and trust that your children are, in general, good judges of character. Many of their friends will be delighted to have a neutral adult in their lives, a counsellor and someone to love on them without having authority over them.

Enter their Music World

If you really want to know a young person you need to know their music playlist. Those songs reflect the things they love and hate, hope for, and fear. In their earlier ages you hopefully screened their music to keep all the bad stuff out. In this stage, you will inevitably have a few discussions about the messages being communicated in their song and movies, but don't forget "Saving All My Love for You" and all the other adultery songs from our own generation. Sin is sin and it's always been reflected in art, from Shakespeare's plays until today.

At this stage in their lives, however, make sure you understand that you are not there to lifeguard them or to police their mindset, but to join them in their world and to gather intelligence to help you understand them better as persons.

Don't you want to know the real truth about your children? If you can't turn off the mother-as-detective program they will simply hide the truth from you and you'll never really know them again. Use self control to wade into their world without judgment as much as you can.

In my parents' generation, teen music was primarily screaming angry rock. Our days as parents aren't nearly as painful. Today's kids have very eclectic tastes in music. They fuse folk music with drums from India. Country has never been bigger and, on the Christian side, young people actually think acoustic hymns are pretty great. There is a renewal of extended worship among Christian youth. Check out Hillsongs United and Bethel Music. Some of the music twenty-year-olds are producing simply makes the soul soar! They know the same God we do.

Whatever your child's taste is, listen to it. Ask them to update your music and teach you about their favorite bands and songs. Get to know their music, and you will know them better. If you want to raise things up another notch, take them and a friend to a concert (after you have learned the words and know about the band). Their friends will think you are so cool and your child will realize how much effort you are exerting to get to know them and the world they occupy.

Time to Share Some Secrets

This is the season for sharing some of the stories about your own life that you might not have revealed before. There are things you have been through that changed you in good ways, and other things that wounded you and left you with regrets. They need to know about this part of your world now, because they are moving toward a day when they will leave your home for college or work and will be subjected to all the things you have tried to protect them from. They need the wisdom that comes from your life experience so they can avoid some of those things in life that might glitter but will also leave them wounded.

It takes a lot of courage to tell your kids the story of your failures and of what you learned from it. Telling these stories can save your children from going through the same heartache you suffered as a result of a poor choice made under pressure.

I once saw this satirical "de-motivational" poster that said, "What if the central purpose of your life is to serve as a warning to others?" That was meant as a joke but really, if telling a story of my own failure helps my children avoid the same fate, then I have actually accomplished much in my life. Why should our children have to make the same mistakes we did, in order to learn the same lessons?

They need to know that they can ask you questions about anything and that you will be forthright with them. They may have some questions about your own marriage or if you ever have doubts about God or the Bible. The time for lectures is over. Now begin the days of adult conversations and your children are far more psychologically advanced than you might think.

These can be fascinating conversations. They may well take you into areas you are uncomfortable in facing. We all have unfinished business and an internal world of stuff that is hidden from others. Our children have a way of ferreting things out and aren't afraid to talk about the elephant in the room. What an apt expression! Imagine having a nice social event where guests mingle in polite conversation. An elephant keeps walking about in the room and nobody is willing to mention it or acknowledge it's problematic existence. Kids won't let that elephant linger long without asking about it. It's refreshing to have such honesty in a relationship. You will never forget some of the conversations you will have with your kids at this age.

Your adolescent may need to unburden themselves of some secrets of their own. Some will be painful for you to hear and may make you feel that you have failed to protect your child. A secret is a heavy thing. They need to get things off their chest sometimes and all they need from us is understanding and acceptance to feel cleansed. You don't need to moralize after they tell you their secret. By their early teens, they are crystal clear about your value system. Just gently encourage them away from the darkness and into paths of light. Encourage is the right word there. That's the primary lever to use in moving them along.

Other revelations won't be intentional confessions. They will just slip out, particularly after their friends become comfortable with you. For example you might be having a normal kitchen conversation, when their friend casually mentions something you didn't know about before. You'll note the tension in your child's body posture and know you've struck information gold. You're going to want to know more about this newly-uncovered secret, but, again, don't freak out and go ballistic on your child. The older they are, the more single incidents of rule-breaking, etc., don't matter nearly as much as keeping the channels of communication open and flowing.

Enter into your child's life in their preteen years and deepen this engagement and the confidential adult tone between you as your child moves toward college age. It's a joyful time of celebrating their continued development and will pave the way for a lifetime mentoring connection into their adulthood.

CHAPTER TWENTY-EIGHT
DRY-DOCKING

In the end, the real secret to every healthy family is healthy parents. As we come to the end of this playbook let's talk about your need for personal and spiritual renewal.

Every ship takes a beating along the journey of its life. The waves bash against it. Salt water works to corrode it. Barnacles—those foreign organisms—attach to it and begin to grow. If unchecked, the barnacles will weigh down the ship and cause drag as it attempts to slice forward through the rough waves. The ship will lose maneuverability because of all these things. Eventually, the perfect storm may come and the little ship be lost upon the rocks.

That's why every shipowner schedules seasons of dry-docking for his ship. It doesn't matter that there are bills to pay or important work to do. The ship must be dry-docked periodically for its own good. The future of the crew and the grand enterprise they are embarked upon depends on the soundness of the ship and the integrity of its hull against anything that might come against it.

Work stops. The ship comes to a dead halt and is pulled with chains from the sea onto a special platform made just for this purpose. First, there is a thorough inventory of the inner and outer workings of the ship. A plan of repair is made. First, those stubborn barnacles are scraped off the hull, no matter how much they resist. All rust is removed. Working parts get cleaned and lubricated. Finally, things are sanded, sealed and repainted. The sleek boat slides gracefully down the rails again and back into the sea for another season of work and adventure.

We are all like that ship. We need scheduled times to evaluate where we are and to note the true condition of our spiritual, emotional and physical health. There will always be barnacles, those contrary, foreign habits and attitudes that have attached themselves firmly to us, making life much more work than it has to be. These have to be addressed regardless of the pain. The presence of barnacles doesn't mean that the ship is bad, just that it has been in the sea for quite a while. The forces of life takes their toll on all of us. No one is above this reality.

Every adult needs to be able to take their own pulse in life. As Jesus put it, "Physician, heal yourself." That's what the Sabbath was all about in God's thinking. It is one day in seven to stop whatever we are doing and renew ourselves for another week.

Sherry and I can't imagine trying to live without our vital connection to God. We need our daily time alone with God. It might be during our commute to work, or by taking a walk to talk things out with Him. We can tune into worship music and sing with all our heart till the cares drop away. This is a fountain of life that we are all invited to enter. Why bear life all alone?

Our Creator has invited us to enter under His covering and to submit and allow Him to be God. He will keep the world spinning properly so we won't have to do that anymore. God has good plans for us and for our children. If you have never really prayed much, we highly recommend the daily habit. Just talk to God as to a perfect Father.

God wants to bless us all but we have to be "blessable." We can't reasonably allow our desires and attitudes to become darkened and still expect Him to make only good things happen to us. If there are things we need to come clean about before Him let's have the courage to do so. He is gracious to forgive when we admit our faults and sins.

Time in the dry-dock can be something we schedule routinely, or something that life will schedule for us through broken relationships, lost employment or a health crisis. As the old maritime proverb says, "He who will not obey the rudder, will obey the rock."

Personal renewal is not optional. Think of the stakes involved. You are the parent, the provider, the secure center of your child's world. As long as you are strong and healthy their support system works. If you flame out or break down in your attitude or become hard-hearted toward a child or your spouse everything is imperiled.

How many divorces could have been prevented if both parents had been healthy emotionally, in shape physically and connected to their spiritual core?

Many family tragedies are simply caused by neglect. The parents and kids were always busy and active but little by little, the most important of things got off balance and wandered farther and farther from the center till the wheels fell off.

This does not have to happen to you. Pace yourself. Establish and maintain a healthy pattern of life.

Healthy Rhythms of Life

The problem with living a balanced life is that the thing won't stay balanced forever. You have to reset it daily or at least weekly.

Weekends, Birthdays, Anniversaries, and holidays like Thanksgiving and New Year's are natural times to take the fearless personal inventory we all need. When you are finished taking your own pulse you can always ask others for feedback as well. Friends who love us can usually show us at least one thing they see that troubles them and makes them worry for our well-being.

If you know, dear friend, that you are well beyond the burnout point and that a weekly sabbath day won't fix what's wrong with you then for everyone's sake, ramp up your care. There was a season in our lives, around our 40th birthday when we had been pushing it too hard for almost a decade. We had done an impressive amount of work. All our kids had been born and were filling up every spare moment of our lives. Everything we had given ourselves to was noble and important. Still, we were becoming empty beyond our ability to be refilled.

We took a month off. It was an unthinkable thought to an American (Aussies and Europeans are laughing right now. They take one every year.). It seemed impossible to do, but how many months or years would be lost if one of us became broken in health or in emotions? We considered it an essential emergency action and made the necessary arrangements at work.

We rented an inexpensive house near a beach and spent thirty days hiking by the sea, watching movies, playing games, drinking hot tea and sleeping, sleeping, sleeping ten hours a day. It saved our ministry and has kept us in the game for the last fifteen years.

There are several programs available like the Emmaeus Walk and other weekend spirituality retreats that would be a good idea for everyone every few years. Just do something, anything, to keep from becoming burned out and broken.

A healthy family is built by healthy adults who raise healthy children. Allowing children to observe your own rhythms of renewal is an important part of training them to stay strong throughout all the seasons coming to their own lives.

Be healthy, dear friend. The next generation is depending on you.

Online Resources

Visit Quinley.com to access the video workshop for Simple Parenting.

AFTERWORD

Honestly, I'm a little sad now that the book is over. I felt that I was somehow just getting to know you, though we may never have met. Each day as I wrote I tried to imagine your daily life as a parent. There is a sameness of sorts in all families, especially in those that strive to become great ones. On my end of these words, I feel that I caught a whisper of your world. We'll be praying for you.

I write something almost every day, but this book was the most difficult writing I have ever attempted. All along I've wondered why. Perhaps it was because family is everything important all rolled into one thing and I felt the burden of trying to do my best for it. Maybe it was something darkly spiritual. Travel around the world and you can't deny a kind of malevolent force raging at all families in every nation. We all love our families and we are battling to keep them whole. Maybe it was just that nothing in my life is more important than serving the Lord in my family, so there were too many things inside my heart that I had to pull single thoughts through, in order to get them to the surface where I could capture them and put them on paper.

Whatever it was, I have done my best with it and now Sherry and I present it to you, dear friend.

If we can be of further help to you we will be that much richer for the opportunity. We'll keep the conversation going on Quinley.com where you will find links to all the other resources we have. If you'd like to contact us directly just write to **chuck@quinley.com** and **sherry@quinley.com**.

May God's blessings be upon your household.

Chuck & Sherry Quinley
June 17, 2014

END NOTES

Sample

MY DAILY WORKSHEET

	ACTION	Points Awarded
✔	Made my bed	
	Picked up my clothes and toys	
✔	Looked everyone in the eye, said "I love you" and gave them a hug.	
✔	Was helpful to Mom	
	Didn't complain even once	
	Brushed my teeth	
✔	Shared with others (Tell us when and with whom)	
	Told myself, "I am strong!"	
	Did something kind for someone else (Tell us what it was please)	
	Read my Bible	

OTHER BOOKS BY CHUCK QUINLEY

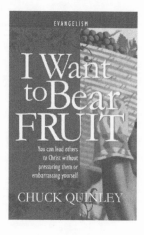

I Want to Bear Fruit: How You Can Share the Gospel Without Pressuring Others or Embarrassing Yourself

Ever feel guilty about your lack of soulwinning? Are you afraid of turning people off in your sincere efforts to lead them to the truth you have found in Christ? This book will show you a simple approach to soul-winning so you can confidently speak only to those who are open and searching for help. No arguing religion. No knocking on doors. If we can just get over our fear of evangelism we can be the ones who bring them out of their spiritual prison and into the arms of their Heavenly Father.

The Quest: A Ten-week Journey into Radical Discipleship

Tired of endless book studies on discipleship? Here is an action-based quest to help you follow Jesus. Inside you will discover 10 Quests Jesus instructed his followers to complete. Do the Quest alone or with a group. Enough talk. Take the challenge. Complete your quest.

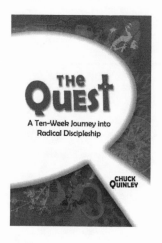

All titles available on Amazon and Kindle.

Contact the author directly for bulk purchases at simpleparentingbook@gmail.com

Made in the USA
San Bernardino, CA
02 August 2014